MASTERING
— YOUR —
CAREER

A Guide from Student to Expert

DR. CHIZARAM NWANKWO

(PhD, AFHEA, C.ErgHF, MCIEHF, Tech.IOSH)

Nancheez Ltd

NANCHEEZ

Copyright

Title: Mastering Your Career: A Guide from Student to Expert

ISBN (Hardcover): 978-1-0687681-0-1
ISBN (Paperback): 978-1-0687681-1-8

Cover Design by: Folahan Agbeyomi
Library of Congress Control Number: [2024913631]
Publisher: Nancheez Ltd
Printed in the United Kingdom

Dedication

To all aspiring professionals,

May this book serve as a guiding light on your journey from student to expert. Your dedication, perseverance, and passion inspire us to reach new heights in our careers. Here is to embrace the path of mastery with courage, determination, and a steadfast commitment to excellence.

With heartfelt dedication,

Dr. Chizaram Nwankwo
(PhD, AFHEA, C.ErgHF, AFHEA, Tech.IOSH)

"Continuous improvement is better than delayed perfection"

Mark Twain

TABLE OF CONTENTS

PREFACE

Welcome to "Mastering Your Career: A Guide from Student to Expert." In today's dynamic and ever-changing career landscape, navigating the journey from student to expert in your chosen field can be both exhilarating and daunting. This book is designed to be your trusted companion along this transformative journey, providing practical insights, actionable strategies, and inspiring stories to help you unlock your full potential and achieve mastery in your career. As you embark on this journey, you must recognise that mastering your career is not just about acquiring technical skills or climbing the corporate ladder. It's about embracing a mindset of continuous growth, learning, and adaptation and cultivating the skills, habits, and attitudes that will enable you to thrive in dynamic professional marketplace.

In "Mastering Your Career," you will explore the critical pillars of career mastery, from setting the foundation and building essential skills to developing expertise, overcoming challenges, and achieving mastery in your chosen field. Each chapter is carefully crafted to address the fundamental aspects of your career journey, offering practical advice, real-world examples, and actionable steps to help you progress towards your goals. Throughout this book, you will encounter stories of how I have navigated my own path from student to expert, facing challenges, seizing opportunities, and ultimately achieving success and fulfilment in my career. I hope my experiences inspire and guide you as you embark on your journey towards mastery.

Whether you are a recent graduate embarking on your career journey, a mid-career professional seeking to level up your skills, or a seasoned expert looking to make a greater impact in your field, "Mastering Your Career" is designed to meet you where you are and provide you with the tools, insights, and inspiration you need to succeed. As you immerse yourself into the chapters ahead, I encourage you to approach this book with an open mind and a willingness to embrace new ideas and perspectives. Take the time to reflect on your own goals, values, and aspirations, and consider how the principles and strategies outlined in this book can help you achieve greater success and fulfilment in your career. Above all, remember that the journey towards career mastery is not a destination but a lifelong pursuit. Embrace the challenges, celebrate the successes, and never stop learning, growing, and evolving professionally. Your journey awaits—so let's embark on this transformative adventure together.

Warm regards,

Dr. Chizaram Nwankwo
(PhD, AFHEA, C.ErgHF, AFHEA, Tech.IOSH)

ACKNOWLEDGEMENTS

Writing a book is never a solitary endeavour, and "Mastering Your Career: A Guide from Student to Expert" is no exception. I am deeply grateful to all those who have contributed to the creation of this book, directly or indirectly, and whose support and encouragement have made this journey possible.

First and foremost, I would like to express my heartfelt gratitude to God Almighty, who gave me the wisdom, knowledge, understanding and life experience I have till date. I would also love to express my appreciation to all the mentors, teachers, and professors who have played a pivotal role in shaping my understanding of the subject matter and inspiring me to pursue excellence in my career. Your guidance, wisdom, and encouragement have been invaluable, and I am profoundly grateful for your support.

I am also indebted to the countless professionals, experts, and thought leaders whose insights and experiences have enriched the content of this book. Your contributions have added depth and perspective to each chapter, and I am honoured to have had the opportunity to learn from your expertise.

A massive thank you to the individuals who generously shared their personal stories and anecdotes, providing real-world examples of the principles and strategies outlined in this book. Your willingness to share your experiences has made this book more relatable and impactful, and I am grateful for your openness and candour.

I want to specially thank my lovely wife, Chisom, who was a constant proofreader of this book, my beautiful daughter, Avielle, my parents, siblings, in-laws and friends for their unwavering support and encouragement throughout the writing process. Your belief in me and your words of encouragement have been a constant source of inspiration, and I am deeply grateful for your love and encouragement.

Last but not least, I want to express my gratitude to the readers of this book. I sincerely hope that the insights and strategies presented in "Mastering Your Career" will empower you to unlock your full potential and achieve success and fulfilment in your chosen career. Thank you for embarking on this journey with me, and I wish you all the best on your path to career mastery.

With heartfelt thanks,

Dr. Chizaram Nwankwo
(PhD, AFHEA, C.ErgHF, AFHEA, Tech.IOSH)

BEFORE YOU DIVE IN

There were certain questions on my mind at various points in my career journey which have been captured in this book. These questions helped me come up with self-help tips in this book which could be pivotal in steering you in the right direction on your journey to mastering your career.

What

-   What should I choose as a career path?

Why

-   Why do I want to do this?

Where

-   Where do I want to do this? Industry sector and/or geographical location

How

-   How can I go about achieving this?

When

-   When can I achieve my dream career goal?

Who

-   Who should I be connecting with as a mentor, and/or who should I be taking on as a mentee?

CHAPTER

ONE

SETTING THE FOUNDATION

UNDERSTANDING YOUR PASSION

Identifying Your Career Path

Introduction

Discovering your passion is the crucial first step towards building a fulfilling career. This section will guide you through the process of self-discovery, helping you identify your interests, values, and strengths to find a career path that aligns with your true calling.

Your beliefs become your thoughts. Your thoughts become your words. Your words become your actions. Your actions become your habits. Your habits become your values. Your values become your destiny."

- Mahatma Gandhi

Exploring Your Interests

Begin by reflecting on the activities and subjects that ignite your curiosity and enthusiasm. What hobbies do you enjoy in your free time? Which topics do you gravitate towards in conversations or when browsing online? Pay attention to the activities that make you lose track of time, as they often indicate areas of genuine interest. The trajectory of my life has been a roller-coaster when it comes to making career choices. I started by applying to study Medicine as an undergraduate at the University of Port Harcourt, Nigeria. However, after an unsuccessful attempt, I went on to Madonna University for a Foundation year. I came back to the University of Port Harcourt, where I started an undergraduate degree in Pharmacy. After studying for three years, I was informed that the course was not accredited and that culminated with poor results. I had to switch to Biochemistry, from which I graduated with a second-class upper degree. I later found myself in the UK studying for a Master's degree in Petroleum and Environmental Technology, after which I graduated with the Best Dissertation/Project, which led me to undertake a PhD in Health and Safety/ Human Factors. My journey demonstrates that your interests can sometimes take a while to manifest in your reality. Still, with determination, perseverance, dedication, and commitment, you will surely attain what you desire.

Identifying Your Values

Consider what matters most to you in life. Your values serve as guiding principles that shape your decisions and actions. Are you motivated by creativity, helping others, or positively impacting society? Reflect on past experiences that have brought you a sense of fulfilment, as they can provide valuable insights into your core values. This was key for me when creating my company values for Nancheez Ltd, a global consultancy firm based in the UK. My tag line states, "transforming lives by providing world-class solutions." It made sense to choose this as it reflects my innate desire to make a positive difference in the world. A considerable part of this process of identifying my values involved introspecting on what brought me utmost satisfaction and which I would be happy doing without even getting paid for it, as well as doing almost effortlessly, or would I say, has become second nature to me. I thrive in helping people and solving complex problems; hence, my career, business and professional life were built around things that align with my value system of providing solutions. "Your beliefs become your thoughts. Your thoughts become your words. Your words become your actions. Your actions become your habits. Your habits become your values. Your values become your destiny." - Mahatma Gandhi.[1]

Assessing Your Strengths

Take stock of your strengths, talents, and natural abilities. What are you good at? What skills do you excel in? Consider technical skills, such as analytical thinking or programming, and soft skills, such as communication or leadership. Reflect on feedback from friends, family, and past experiences to better understand your strengths. During my school days, I was always this bookworm, top-of-the-class

---

[1] Avadhesh Kumar Singh, 'Gandhian Values in the 21 St Century', *Indian Literature* 63, no. 5 (313 (2019): 163–72.

kind of guy. However, after lots of ups and downs during my academic journey, there came a point in my life where I lost my zeal and enthusiasm for education, and it took some reminding from family and friends for me to realise my strengths and get back to winning ways. Trust me, confidence sometimes constitutes over 90% of what you need to harness your strengths. I say that people who have confidence in their abilities have already rigged the system against those who do not. According to Marcus Garvey, "If you have no confidence in self, you are twice defeated in the race of life." What are those things you are extremely good at? What do people tell you that you are great at? What can you do without too much cognitive demand? What is that thing you do better than those around you? In there lies your strength and what sets you apart from everyone else. Focus on these things and play down your weaknesses. My career in human factors has taught me that to achieve the best performance out of a human-centred system, you must design the system in such a way that it harnesses our strengths and limits our weaknesses, which makes it easier for us to do the right thing and difficult to do the wrong thing[2], and that in turn stirs up confidence.

Exploring Career Options

Once you better understand your interests, values, and strengths, begin exploring potential career paths that align with them. Research different industries, job roles, and organisations to identify opportunities that resonate with you. Take advantage of

---

[2] M Sanders and JMC Cormick, 'Human Factors in Engineering and Design. New York: McHill', 1993.

informational interviews, job shadowing, and online resources to gain insights into various career paths. For me, especially as an international student who came to the UK with no work experience within the country, it was always an uphill task to land my dream job immediately. I should state that this is the mistake I find many international students or immigrants into new terrains or countries make when they come in first. They are keen to hit the ground running in their chosen career path and start applying for highly skilled jobs from the moment they get in. However, after multiple rejections due to inadequate work experience, frustration sets in, which could quickly douse confidence. Rather than focus solely on your chosen career path, there is nothing wrong with picking up menial jobs around warehouse operations, care giving, customer service, tutoring, etc., to help you gain much-needed transferable skills that could be pivotal in creating a pathway for you to land your dream job. Also, I encourage new entrants into any country to come in with some handy skills such as tailoring, cooking, carpentry, plumbing, cleaning, etc., as these could help you settle in quickly and earn some money while exploring potential career options. During the career exploration process, ensure you note how lucrative your career path is in your chosen country of residence and what progression looks like within your industry sector. I ensured that I got stuck with consistent research into various industry sectors and job roles to see what aligns with my passion or interests and what puts food on the table. Yes!!! You need money to fuel your passion; NEVER FORGET THAT!

Testing and Experimenting

Don't be afraid to try new things and experiment with different career options. Internships, volunteer work, and part-time jobs can provide valuable hands-on experience and help you test the waters before committing to a particular path. Keep an open mind and be willing to pivot if you discover that a certain career path isn't the right fit for you. Sometimes, this can come at a huge cost, such as taking certification courses, travelling for conferences, applying for multiple jobs (with rejections), etc. Nonetheless, these should not dissuade you from keeping your foot on the throttle and pressing on till you find where your passion meets your purpose. There were times I applied for hundreds of jobs daily and received almost the same number of rejections. You know, the emails come in with a nice statement of how well your profile suits the job role, and the next paragraph starts with, unfortunately. I got so used to it that I would normally not read the entire email and just head over to the second paragraph. This series of rejections then led me to deviate from applying for job roles where I needed to fill in long application forms online to start applying for "Easy-Apply" roles where I just needed to upload my CV and apply with a single click on job board portals such as Indeed, CV Library, Total Jobs, LinkedIn etc. However, the drawback of the One-Click application system is that the same way you apply is exactly how hundreds of other people apply for the same role. Therefore, the probability of landing that role is next to impossible, considering you are up against many people whose profiles might have suited the advertised job role better than yourself. I advocate for quality over quantity regarding job applications, even if I know this could sometimes be draining. However, by properly filling out detailed job applications, you also get to truly understand what the company wants and how you can fit into that role with your current skills. You also have the opportunity to reflect on your own work experience to see deficient areas where you can improve.

Furthermore, the competition is less stiff when making long applications. I reckon this is a measure employers apply to filter out unserious candidates who are not passionate about the role. So, feel free to experiment and be dogged with it. Don't give up!!!

Reflecting and Refining

As you explore different career options, take time to reflect on your experiences and how they align with your interests, values, and strengths. What aspects of a job do you enjoy the most? What tasks or environments do you find most challenging or fulfilling? Use this feedback to refine your understanding of your passion and narrow down your career options. Job seekers often look for what they can offer the organisation they are applying to. However, they rarely examine how the company itself can benefit them. When you apply for a job, I want you to remember that the employer is looking for how your skills can help them achieve their missions and vision, and you should equally be looking for how that organisation can help you achieve yours. Whether it is a particular expected salary, bonus perks, pension schemes, work-life balance, or company profile, you must identify what matters to you in your career and personal life. In my own case, I have placed a lot of value on my work-life balance as I know I have much to offer the world apart from what I do for work. I had always loved the idea of working from home, even before the COVID-19 pandemic. Also, maybe due to my PhD programme, I am more productive when working alone, but this is not to say I am not a team player. You may find that you are more of a social butterfly who might love the idea of an open-plan office setting. Again, different strokes for different folks. The most important thing is ensuring that any organisation you will be getting involved with matches your values and interests and is a good fit for you, as you are to them. Put yourself first!!!

Summary

Identifying your passion is a journey of self-discovery that requires introspection, exploration, and reflection. Understanding your interests, values, and strengths can pave the way for a career that brings you joy, fulfilment, and success. Embrace the process with an open mind and trust that the path to your dream career will unfold before you.

Career Mastery Exercise

Exploring Your Interests

1. **Reflect on Activities:** List at least five activities or hobbies that you enjoy doing in your free time. Note why they captivate you and how they make you feel.
2. **Curiosity Journal:** Keep a journal for a week, noting any topics or activities that pique your interest or make you lose track of time.
3. **Conversation Topics:** Identify three topics you frequently discuss with enthusiasm. Reflect on why these subjects are important to you.

Identifying Your Values

1. **Value Inventory:** Write down the top five values that are most important to you (e.g., creativity, helping others, financial stability). Consider how these values influence your decisions.
2. **Fulfilment Reflection:** Recall a moment in your life when you felt most fulfilled. Describe the experience and identify the values it reflects.
3. **Value Alignment:** Compare your list of values with your current career or life choices. Are they in alignment? If not, what changes could you make?

Assessing Your Strengths

1. **Skill Assessment:** List your top five strengths or skills. Include both technical and soft skills.
2. **Feedback Loop:** Ask three friends or family members to identify what they believe are your strengths. Compare their feedback with your self-assessment.
3. **Strength Utilization:** Reflect on a recent project or task where you utilised your strengths. How did it contribute to your success?

Exploring Career Options

1. **Industry Research:** Select three industries of interest. Research each one, focusing on job roles, required skills, and growth opportunities.
2. **Informational Interviews:** Schedule at least one informational interview per industry with professionals currently working in those fields.

3. **Job Shadowing:** Seek opportunities to job shadow or volunteer in roles that interest you to gain firsthand experience.

Testing and Experimenting

1. **Internship/Volunteer:** Apply for internships, volunteer positions, or part-time jobs in areas related to your interests and values.
2. **Side Projects:** Start a side project or freelance work in a field you're interested in to gain practical experience.
3. **Skill Development:** Enrol in a course or workshop to develop a skill that aligns with your career interests.

Reflecting and Refining

1. **Experience Reflection:** After trying new roles or projects, reflect on what aspects you enjoyed the most and what you found challenging.
2. **Feedback Session:** Discuss your experiences with a mentor or career coach to gain insights and advice.
3. **Career Alignment:** Regularly revisit your interests, values, and strengths to ensure your career path remains aligned with your evolving self-discovery.

RESEARCHING YOUR FIELD

— • —

*Learning About Industry
Trends and Demands*

Introduction

In the 21st century's dynamic and evolving job market, staying informed about industry trends and demands is essential for career success. This section will equip you with strategies and resources to conduct effective research in your chosen field, helping you stay ahead of the curve and make informed decisions about your career path.

> *"You can go as far as you want, but you will have to walk as long as you do not want."*

Understanding Industry Landscape

Begin by gaining a comprehensive understanding of the broader landscape of your industry. What are the key sectors, companies, and players within your field? What are the major trends, challenges, and opportunities shaping the industry? Conducting a thorough analysis of industry reports, market analyses, and news articles can provide valuable insights into the current state of your field. Before going into health and safety as a career, I had to understand the job possibilities and how my career path would pan out. While my dissertation during my MSc degree in Petroleum and Environmental Technology focused on developing a health and safety framework for the oil and gas industry, the breadth of knowledge I attained from conducting the research meant that I was versatile in applying my health and safety knowledge across a wide array of industry sectors.

Identifying Emerging Trends

Stay abreast of emerging trends and innovations shaping your industry's future. Attend industry conferences, seminars, and webinars to learn about the latest developments and advancements. Engage with thought leaders, influencers, and experts in your field through networking events and online communities to gain insider perspectives on upcoming trends and technologies. My university supervisors were instrumental in helping me sign up to attend various health and safety conferences worldwide, which, to date, even in my current workplace, I still attend yearly. A key developmental factor in my career has been my ability to network at these conferences and seminars, which, in fact, led me to meet one of my mentors who landed me my current role. So, in terms of career growth, ensure that you consistently pursue knowledge on current trends within your industry sector as this could be a great conversation starter for networking with like-minded professionals.

Analysing Skills and Job Demand

Research the specific skills and qualifications in high demand within your industry. Analyse job postings, job descriptions, and LinkedIn profiles of professionals in your field to identify common skill sets and requirements. Pay attention to emerging job roles, specialisations gaining traction, and technical skills and certifications that employers value. I earlier referred to a period when I kept on applying for hundreds of jobs daily only to receive "unfortunately" emails in return consistently. This continued for years until I had to take a step back to analyse what I was doing wrong. I realised that I was not selling myself as much as I should have been. I had a wealth of relevant skills, which I should have highlighted in my CV and cover letters coherently, using keywords that the employer sought. However, based on what sounded good to me, I was set in my ways of applying for jobs. It was not until I started taking various certification courses and enhancing my interpersonal skills that I received many interview invitations and job offers. Always remember that the job description is already a pointer as to what your CV should look like. There is nothing wrong with tailoring your CV with the relevant skills to match the job descriptions for the role you wish to apply for. However, ensure you do not include false information in your CV, as this will only go on to dent your credibility. Instead, if there are skills or certifications for a job you are after that you do not have, work on getting those skills and include in your CV that you are working towards them. Employers will appreciate your honesty and dedication to continuous improvement.

Exploring Career Trajectories

Examine the various career trajectories and pathways available within your industry. What are the typical career progression routes for professionals in your field? Are there alternative career paths or niche roles that align with your interests and strengths? Conduct informational interviews with professionals at different stages of their careers to gain insights into their career journeys and decision-making processes. When asked by my mentees about how much they could progress in a chosen career path, I always tell them, "You can go as far as you want, but you will have to walk as long as you do not want." Career progression is an open cheque in which you determine the amount you put on it. Never think you have reached a brick wall or ceiling in your career development. As a matter of fact, when you stay too long at a particular level, a part of your brain that stimulates innovation and creativity (hippocampus) starts getting smaller and less functional [3], which means you stifle your growth as a professional. Always seek new ways to add soft skills in management, leadership, organisation, public speaking, etc., as well as hard skills related to your chosen career path. That is what makes you relevant even in thirty years to come. Think about it: in about thirty years, at the rate the world is

---

[3] Roger E. Beaty, 'The Creative Brain', *Cerebrum: The Dana Forum on Brain Science* 2020 (1 January 2020): cer-02-20.

going, more jobs will be lost to AI and robots, so you need to do all you can to make yourself relevant in any job dispensation.

Seeking Mentorship and Guidance

Seek mentorship and guidance from seasoned professionals who can provide valuable insights and advice based on their industry experience. Reach out to mentors, industry veterans, and alumni from your educational institution or professional network to solicit feedback and guidance. Establishing meaningful connections with mentors can offer invaluable support and guidance as you navigate your career path. Mentors have played a major role in my career development to date. I have had mentors in academia, industry, religion, cognitive mental development, marriage, family, finance management, and every other facet of life. You are unlikely to make a mistake if you speak to someone who has made that journey before you. Mentors are like maps or satellite navigation that show you the destination you need to get to and how to get there. Having a mentor can reduce a journey of ten years to a few months. I can choose to drive a hundred miles to a certain destination, but without a map to get there, I might be going a hundred miles in the opposite direction, which means by the time I realise it and decide to use a map, I might have to travel back two hundred miles to my initial destination. The longer you delay having a mentor, the longer it might take you to reach your desired goal or achieve your dream. Get a mentor today but ensure that your chosen mentor is someone you respect and trust, has been there and done it, can constructively critique you were necessary, and has a positive mindset and can-do attitude.

Utilising Online Resources

Take advantage of online resources and tools to stay informed about industry trends and demands. Subscribe to industry newsletters, blogs, and podcasts to receive regular updates and insights from industry experts. Follow relevant hashtags and accounts on social media platforms like Twitter and LinkedIn to stay connected with your field's latest news and discussions. Social media is an instrumental tool for accessing essential information regarding career opportunities and developmental pathways for professionals. However, many young people spend their entire day on social media, which is not necessarily bad, but what you are doing on there is what makes it right or wrong. If all you do is listen to gossip from blogs about other people and less content on what will develop and build you as a person, you are already headed for failure. Is it not funny that the algorithms that guide TikTok feeds in the Western World are more geared towards trending dancing videos, funny clips, skits, etc... At the same time, those in countries like China, such as Douyin, are more tailored towards technology, innovation, and creativity?[4] You can start building your dreams today or watch others on social media build theirs. The choice is yours: "Watch or Be Watched!!!"

---

[4] Yang Yang, 'TikTok/Douyin Use and Its Influencer Video Use: A Cross-Cultural Comparison between Chinese and US Users', *Online Media and Global Communication* 1, no. 2 (2022): 339–68.

Summary

Researching your field is a continuous process that requires diligence, curiosity, and proactive engagement. By staying informed about industry trends and demands, you can position yourself as a knowledgeable and competitive professional in your field. Embrace lifelong learning and adaptability as you navigate your industry's dynamic landscape and use research to empower your career growth and success.

Career Mastery Exercise

Understanding Industry Landscape

1. **Industry Research:** Dedicate time each week to read industry reports, market analyses, and news articles. Create a summary of key trends, challenges, and opportunities shaping your field.
2. **Sector Analysis:** Identify and list the key sectors, companies, and players within your industry. Understand their roles and how they influence the market.
3. **Case Study:** Conduct a case study on a major company in your industry. Analyse its growth, challenges, and strategies for success.

Identifying Emerging Trends

1. **Conference Participation:** Sign up for at least one industry conference, seminar, or webinar. Take notes on the latest developments and advancements.
2. **Networking:** Engage with thought leaders and influencers in your field through LinkedIn, professional networks, and

industry events. Start by sending a connection request with a personalised message to at least three professionals.

3. **Trend Tracking:** Create a list of emerging trends and technologies. Regularly update this list as you discover new information and insights.

Analysing Skills and Job Demand

1. **Job Posting Review:** Analyse job postings for your desired roles. Identify the common skills, qualifications, and certifications that are frequently mentioned.

2. **Skill Gap Analysis:** Compare the required skills with your current skill set. Identify gaps and create a plan to acquire these skills through courses, workshops, or certifications.

3. **Professional Profiles:** Review LinkedIn profiles of successful professionals in your field. Note the skills, experiences, and endorsements they have.

Exploring Career Trajectories

1. **Career Path Mapping:** Research the typical career progression routes in your industry. Create a visual map of potential pathways and roles that interest you.

2. **Informational Interviews:** Schedule informational interviews with professionals at different stages of their careers. Prepare questions about their career journeys, challenges, and advice for newcomers.

3. **Alternative Roles:** Explore niche roles or alternative career paths that align with your interests and strengths. Research what it takes to transition into these areas.

Seeking Mentorship and Guidance

1. **Mentor Identification:** Identify potential mentors within your network or industry. Consider reaching out to alumni from your educational institution or professionals you've met at events.
2. **Mentor Outreach:** Craft a respectful and concise message to potential mentors explaining why you seek their guidance and how you admire their career path.
3. **Regular Check-Ins:** Establish regular meetings with your mentor to discuss your progress, seek advice, and adjust your career strategy as needed.

Utilising Online Resources

1. **Subscribe to Newsletters:** Sign up for industry newsletters, blogs, and podcasts. Dedicate time each week to read or listen to these resources and summarise key takeaways.
2. **Social Media Engagement:** Follow relevant hashtags and accounts on Twitter and LinkedIn. Participate in discussions and share your insights to build your online presence.
3. **Online Learning:** Enrol in online courses or attend webinars related to your field. Dedicate time each week to enhance your knowledge and skills.

SETTING CLEAR GOALS

*Establishing Short-Term and
Long-Term Objectives*

Introduction

Goal setting is the foundation of success in any endeavour, including your career. In this section, we'll explore the importance of setting clear and actionable goals, both in the short-term and long-term, to drive your career forward and achieve your aspirations.

> *"Having a strong value system and "why" that goes beyond yourself and adds value to humanity influences your motivation and drive in your chosen career path."*

Understanding the Power of Goals

Goals provide direction, focus, and motivation in your career journey. They help you clarify your aspirations, prioritise your efforts, and track your progress over time. Setting specific, measurable, achievable, relevant, and time-bound (SMART) goals allows you to create a roadmap for success and hold yourself accountable for your actions. Let me be honest — I have always been the type of person whose life has taken a trajectory very different from what I initially anticipated; however, it always ends up better than I would have imagined if it had gone my own way. As I mentioned earlier, I initially had a dream to study Medicine, ended up in Pharmacy, and changed to Biochemistry, where I finished my first-degree. I had no plans to come to the UK but ended up being here, and I thought I maybe would go for an Oil and Gas Master's degree as I was exhausted with the thought of pursuing a medical degree. A few days into the course, it seemed like I had made the wrong decision, as I had no clue what they were talking about. When I approached one of my lecturers to ask if I could quit the course and return to Nigeria, he said people like me always have the best results. Not only did I have the highest score in that module, but the same lecturer became my dissertation supervisor, where I won an award for Best Dissertation in the Faculty of Engineering at Coventry University, which led me to do my PhD on that same topic. This is what kickstarted my Health and Safety career, and despite thinking it would be in the oil and gas industry, I found myself in a health and safety role at Public Health England (now the UK Health Security Agency), a healthcare industry sector. This job was initially the least in the pecking order of my goals and aspirations; however, it turned out to be the best decision I ever made, as the contacts I have made from being in that organisation have proven invaluable to my career progression to date. Therefore, be sure to set clear and SMART goals, but also be open-minded that it might not always go as you planned, but it always ends up better so long as you keep pushing.

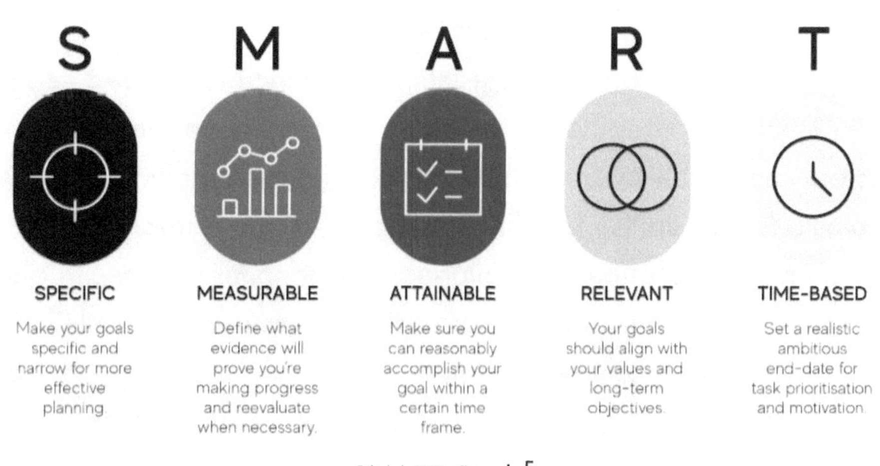

SMART Goals[5]

Identifying Your Values and Priorities

Start by reflecting on your core values, passions, and priorities in life. What matters most to you? What are your long-term aspirations and dreams? Align your goals with your values and priorities to ensure they resonate with your authentic self and contribute to your happiness and fulfilment. When I discovered health and safety as a career, I had to ask myself some difficult questions. Why am I doing this, and what is the greater purpose and meaning I derive

---

[5] Future Learn, 'SMART Goals and Effectiveness', *FutureLearn* (blog), accessed 8 August 2024, https://www.futurelearn.com/info/blog.

from this? These questions led me to my ultimate vision for my career, as they also embodied my values, which were to transform lives positively. In my home country, Nigeria, health and safety are not a top priority and are far from being embedded in our culture as a nation. This shortcoming is reflected in the policies or lack thereof regarding health and safety legislation and the consequences of not adhering to safety practices. Over the years, the country has had several catastrophic events due to a lack of adequate health and safety legislation, guidance, approved codes of practices and regulatory enforcement across various industry sectors and organisations. These incidents, which include pipeline explosions, oil spills, building collapses, road traffic incidents, plane crashes, occupational injuries, and long-term ill health due to hazardous chemical and radioactive exposures, have claimed tons of lives and properties and negatively impacted the livelihoods of the Nigerian people.[6] This has been a driving factor in my motivation to not only be the best in my career but benchmark best practices from countries such as the UK, where health and safety are at the heart of all they do, and integrate these factors to influence policy setting and decision-making at the federal, state and local governments levels of my home country, as well as the legislature, executive and judicial arms of government. I strongly believe that if I can provide adequate justification of implementing robust health and safety legislations to the nation's leadership in terms of the financial, moral, and legal benefits it will provide for the nation, it could go a long way in fostering collaboration at all levels and encourage public and private sector buy-in into the

---

[6] Nnedinma Umeokafor et al., 'Enforcement of Occupational Safety and Health Regulations in Nigeria: An Exploration', *European Scientific Journal* 3 (2014): 93–104.

initiative. Having a strong value system and "why" that goes beyond yourself and adds value to humanity influences your motivation and drive in your chosen career path.

Establishing Long-Term Objectives

Define the long-term objectives or "big picture" goals you aspire to achieve throughout your career. These may include milestones such as reaching a specific position, earning a certain salary, or making a meaningful impact in your industry. Break down these long-term goals into smaller, manageable steps to make them more attainable and actionable. My health and safety consultancy, Nancheez Ltd, was birthed from the long-term vision of owning a conglomerate that provides solutions across various industry sectors. This dream has been fuelled by having a big picture, which again enhances my motivation to look forward to something bigger than myself that will positively transform lives globally.

Nonetheless, you risk feeling disillusioned and demotivated if you set unrealistic goals. Ensure that you set long-term goals that are not only SMART but committed and driven to achieve. This is why your "why" is important because in your journey to achieving your long-term goals, you will meet what I call roadblocks, and the major factor that will make you get past them is the strength of your "why," the purpose behind that vision. The stronger the purpose, the more likely you will stay the course when the journey does not look so promising.

Setting Short-Term Milestones

Create short-term milestones or objectives as stepping stones towards your long-term goals. These may include acquiring new skills, completing certifications, gaining relevant experience, or expanding your professional network. Break down your short-term goals into weekly, monthly, or quarterly targets to maintain momentum and track your progress consistently. On your journey to achieving long-term goals, it is also important to set short-term goals. One major reason for this is that it not only provides you assuredness in reaching long-term goals but is also a motivating factor in the not-so-good days for you to look back on and see how far you have come.

Additionally, short-term goals offer you a consistent reward scheme to know that you have achieved a good number of successes along the way while giving you an overview of where you are on your journey to long-term success. They also help you set these SMART objectives by working in an agile manner, which means that you can easily adapt to any changes, and if anything does not go according to plan, you do not have to retrace your steps a long way backwards to get things right. You must take a trip back to the last short-term goal you set and work your way back from there. Think of it like a video game with various checkpoints where you can save the progress of how far you have gone in the game. Imagine you did not have this feature and got killed on the stage just before the game's final level and had to start all over again. Discouraging, isn't it? That is why short-term goals are an irreplaceable component of goal setting.

Making Goals Specific and Measurable

Ensure that your goals are specific and measurable, with clear criteria for success. Instead of vague aspirations like "get promoted," define specific criteria such as "earn a promotion to a senior management position within the next three years." Break down larger goals into smaller, actionable tasks with measurable outcomes to track your progress effectively. It is one thing to set a goal and another thing to work towards your goal. A key thing to note here is that the first thing that will derail you from achieving your desired goal is how vague or ambiguous your objectives are set. I usually say to university students I supervise during their dissertation projects to ensure that they set SMART objectives because you cannot solve the entire problems of the world. If a student says in their dissertation objectives, "I want to increase company profitability"; well, it sounds good, doesn't it? I mean, who doesn't want that? But the issue here is, because you have failed to specify what metric you want to improve in terms of company profitability, how you intend to do this, and by how much you want to improve this, you will find yourself roaming about almost aimlessly without a defined target to aim for. The same thing applies to your career. Set goals that are specific, measurable, achievable, relevant and time-bound.

Creating Accountability and Accountability Systems

Hold yourself accountable for achieving your goals by establishing accountability systems and mechanisms. Share your goals with trusted friends, family members, or mentors who can provide support, encouragement, and feedback along the way. Regularly review your progress, celebrate your successes, and adjust your goals to stay on track. At the start of every year, everyone comes up with fantastic New Year resolutions: starting that business, going to the gym, eating healthier, taking that certification course, getting a new job, etc. However, give it till the end of January, and those resolutions start getting bleaker by the day until you fall even farther away from when you started. Trust me; I am speaking from experience as well. The first ever time I went to the gym was with friends, and I observed that at the initial stage, it did give me the added motivation to go in the first place. More importantly, it also gave me the zeal to go even harder when doing exercises, especially during times when I may not have been able to do that last rep, set, or workout routine on my own. It pays to have someone who can hold you accountable to the goals you have set. This does not necessarily have to be a mentor, but it should be someone whose advice you will take seriously and act on. There is no need to have an accountability partner that you will hardly listen to. Stay around positive people who will remind you of your why's and even help you shape, define, and refine them. We all need a shoulder to lean on for strength when things might not be as rosy as they were when we started, and not having a positive-minded voice or having a negative one can put a stop to your progress altogether.

Maintaining Flexibility and Adaptability

While setting clear goals is important, remaining flexible and adaptable in changing circumstances is also essential. Be open to revising your goals based on new opportunities, challenges, or insights that arise along your career journey. Embrace failure as a learning opportunity and adjust your course as needed to stay aligned with your evolving aspirations. Think of it as a satellite navigation set up to take you from point A to B. However, along the way, the satellite navigation might detect that there is an even better route than earlier anticipated and will then reroute your journey. You might seem unsure at first, but it might end up saving you from unforeseen roadblocks ahead or offering you better alternative routes which would save you time on your journey. I used my situation early on in my career as an example. Almost all my goals might have not been achieved as I initially desired. In fact, my goals have changed drastically from when I started, and this is because sometimes, we do not even know or are sure of what we want in the first place. Remember I said I initially wanted to study Medicine. Ask me why — because I loved the look of a laboratory coat on a doctor and how smart they looked to have solutions to patient's problems. But is that "why" strong enough to keep me going when things are unplanned? I think the answer is evident in the outcome of where I am today. The funny thing is that even if I became a doctor, I might not have been fulfilled or satisfied in that career path today. So sometimes, fate does present you with alternatives that are better than your selected choice. You must be sensitive, discerning, and brave enough to make risky decisions without focusing too much on the adverse effects of things that could happen if things do not go well. Think more from a position of success than failure, enhancing your risk appetite, innovation, and creativity.

Summary

Setting clear goals is fundamental to achieving success and fulfilment in your career. By establishing short-term and long-term objectives aligning with your values and priorities, you can create a roadmap for progress and growth. Stay focused, stay motivated, and stay committed to pursuing your goals with passion and determination.

Career Mastery Exercise

Understanding the Power of Goals

1. **Clarify Aspirations:** Write down your long-term career aspirations. Be as specific as possible about what you want to achieve and why it matters to you.
2. **Set SMART Goals:** Develop at least three SMART (Specific, Measurable, Achievable, Relevant, Time-bound) goals for your career. For example, "Earn a promotion to a senior management position within the next three years."
3. **Create a Roadmap:** Break down your long-term goals into smaller, manageable steps. Outline the actions you need to take to achieve each goal and set deadlines for each step.

Identifying Your Values and Priorities

1. **Core Values Reflection:** List your top five core values. Reflect on how these values influence your career decisions and goals.
2. **Passion and Priorities:** Write down your passions and priorities. Consider how your career can align with these aspects to ensure fulfilment and happiness.

3. **Align Goals with Values:** Review your career goals and ensure they align with your core values and priorities. Adjust your goals if necessary to reflect what truly matters to you.

Establishing Long-Term Objectives

1. **Big Picture Goals:** Define your long-term career objectives, such as reaching a specific position, earning a particular salary, or making a significant impact in your industry.
2. **Break Down Objectives:** Divide your long-term goals into smaller, actionable steps. Create a timeline for achieving each step, ensuring they lead you towards your ultimate objectives.
3. **Visualisation Exercise:** Create a vision board or write a detailed description of your ideal career scenario. Use this as motivation and a reminder of your long-term goals.

Setting Short-Term Milestones

1. **Weekly Targets:** Set weekly targets that contribute to your long-term goals. These can include tasks such as completing a certification course, attending a networking event, or updating your CV.
2. **Monthly Goals:** Establish monthly goals that serve as stepping stones towards your larger objectives. Track your progress and adjust your plan as needed.
3. **Quarterly Reviews:** Conduct quarterly reviews of your goals and milestones. Assess your progress, celebrate your achievements, and make any necessary adjustments.

Making Goals Specific and Measurable

1. **Detail Your Goals:** Ensure your goals are specific and measurable. For example, instead of "improve skills," specify "complete an advanced Excel course by the end of the month."
2. **Success Criteria:** Define clear criteria for success for each goal. This will help you track your progress and know when you have achieved your objective.
3. **Action Plan:** Create a detailed action plan for each goal, outlining the steps you need to take and the resources you will need. Set deadlines for each step.

Creating Accountability and Accountability Systems

1. **Accountability Partner:** Share your goals with a trusted friend, family member, or mentor who can provide support, encouragement, and feedback.
2. **Regular Check-ins:** Schedule regular check-ins with your accountability partner to discuss your progress and any challenges you face.
3. **Progress Tracking:** Keep a journal or use a goal-tracking app to monitor your progress. Celebrate your successes and learn from any setbacks.

Maintaining Flexibility and Adaptability

1. **Regular Reflection:** Take time to reflect on your goals and progress regularly. Be open to adjusting your goals based on new opportunities or challenges.

2. **Embrace Failure:** View failures as learning opportunities. Reflect on what went wrong, what you can learn from the experience, and how you can adjust your approach.
3. **Stay Open-minded:** Be flexible and adaptable in your career journey. Embrace new opportunities and be willing to pivot if necessary to stay aligned with your evolving aspirations.

TWO

BUILDING SKILLS

CONTINUOUS LEARNING

Embracing Lifelong Education and Skill Development

Introduction

In a world that is consistently changing, continuous learning is no longer just a choice but a necessity for staying relevant and competitive in your career. This section explores the importance of embracing lifelong education and skill development to adapt to evolving industry demands and unlock new opportunities for growth and advancement.

> *"The day you stop learning is the day you start dying."*
>
> **- Albert Einstein**

The Need for Lifelong Learning

The pace of technological innovation and industry disruption requires professionals to continually update their knowledge and skills to remain competitive in the job market. Lifelong learning enhances your expertise and fosters adaptability, resilience, and agility in navigating career transitions and challenges. Continuing Professional Development (CPD) has been a key metric for assessing how far I have come and to help me refine my goals for the future in my chosen career path. I have constantly dedicated and committed to learning one new skill each year: either in the form of a certification course, an aptitude, hard or soft skills, transferrable skills, management and leadership skills, etc. As part of my CPD, I get to log any planned, ongoing or completed professional activities on my record and based on what I have filled in, the system generates a personal development plan for me to highlight my areas of strengths and weaknesses. This helps me not only understand what I need to work on, but also creates a track record and evidence of my professional achievements which serve as an excellent reflective piece. According to the great inventor Albert Einstein, "The day you stop learning is the day you start dying."

Embracing a Growth Mindset

Developing a growth mindset is essential for embracing lifelong learning. Cultivate a belief that your abilities can be developed through dedication and hard work rather than being fixed traits. Embrace challenges, seek feedback, and view setbacks as opportunities for growth and learning. Think back to a moment where you failed in some venture you were undertaking, maybe at school, a business, a job, a project, or even in family life. Now, reflect on one moment where you learned from this failure and applied it to become better at it. How rewarding did it feel at the end? In life, success and failure are not destinations but experiences on your path to greatness, which ultimately shape your destiny, for better or worse. However, the journey's end is determined by your character during tests and trials or in uncomfortable or unfamiliar situations. You cannot get promoted to a new class year without first passing a series of tests or examinations. The same principle applies in life; you cannot expect to grow to a new height in your career without experiencing dips along the way. Those dips give an interesting story to your life, just like the thrill that comes with last-minute winners in sports or a suspense thriller movie with a happy ending. Embrace that growth mindset and see how far you can unlock your potential.

Exploring Diverse Learning Opportunities

Expand your horizons by exploring diverse learning opportunities beyond traditional education channels. Enrol in online courses, webinars, workshops, and seminars to acquire new knowledge and skills. Leverage educational platforms like Coursera, Udemy, and LinkedIn Learning to access courses tailored to your interests and career goals. I have been a massive beneficiary of online courses that cut across my specific field and many other disciplines. I have learnt Project Management courses such as Waterfall, Agile, Scrum Master, and Product Owner; IT courses such as Python, SQL, Power BI, Microsoft Excel, and SPSS; Health and Safety topics such as HAZOP, SHERPA, HAZID, SEIPS, etc. all from online courses. The best news is that many of these courses are free nowadays, but even if they are paid, the biggest investment you can make in your life is in yourself. Think of it this way: if all you had in terms of material wealth and possessions were stripped off you today, and you were to start life all over in a new land where you knew nobody, would you survive? The survival skills that will get you back on your feet in no time is what you have in your head, not just in your bank account. The stuff you are made of is what defines you as a person and, in fact, produces the result of what most people think defines them; "MONEY."

Seeking Mentorship and Guidance

Seek mentorship and guidance from experienced professionals who can provide valuable insights and advice based on their industry experience. Mentorship relationships offer opportunities for knowledge sharing, skill development, and career guidance, helping you navigate challenges and capitalise on opportunities in your career journey. I have spoken previously about the importance of having mentors in your career journey. I have also alluded to the important roles of mentors in helping me identify and succeed in my chosen career path. I have also reiterated it is great to take online courses to develop yourself; however, one thing you do not want to do is to be shooting aimlessly without a goal. You might undertake 500 courses that do not align with your ultimate vision and purpose, and instead of this being a motivation and inspiration in your career, it might very well just make you give up. I have come across tons of people, most of who are my mentees today, who were on the brink of giving up their dreams and changing career paths because they felt it was no longer for them, as they were not reaping any fruits from their hard labour. No job interviews, let alone job offers. However, after having some 1-2-1 mentorship sessions with them, it was evident that there was no clear developmental pathway to help them reach the peak of their careers, and this was exacerbated by the lack of a mentor in their lives. Remember, a good mentor is a catalyst that speeds up the reaction of your career goals and shortens your journey by years.

Building a Personal Learning Network

Build a personal learning network (PLN) of peers, mentors, and industry experts who can support your learning journey. Engage in professional networking events, online communities, and social media platforms to connect with like-minded professionals, share resources, and exchange ideas. Collaborate with others to foster a culture of continuous learning and collective growth. Every year, I attend networking events and conferences where I meet like-minded professionals and experts who have already reached and even surpassed my dreams. Guess what that does? It helps refine my overall vision and see that I can even dream bigger. When we share our experiences of not just our successes but our failures, we pick vital lessons from one another and find a better workaround for various projects we may be struggling with. Peer learning is highly underrated, and I suggest you build a network of professionals who inspire you and are inspired by you, which will create a rollercoaster effect and a win-win situation for all parties.

Applying Learning in Real-world Contexts

Apply your learning in real-world contexts to reinforce retention and mastery of new skills. Seek opportunities for hands-on projects, internships, and experiential learning experiences that allow you to practise and apply what you've learned. Reflect on your experiences, identify areas for improvement, and iterate on your approach to deepen your understanding and expertise. For someone who has about a decade of working experience in academia, I will posit that a major flaw in most curricula is the lack of practical application of theories and frameworks in real-world contexts. It is one thing to hypothesise about how to do something, but it is another thing to do it. According to Bloom's Taxonomy of Learning[7], learning starts from remembering, understanding, applying, analysing, evaluating, and creating. Therefore, it is imperative that as someone on their way to career mastery, your vision should be to create something valuable out of what you have learned. There is a saying, "The richest place in the world is the graveyard because that is where you have the most dreams that never materialise." Build your dreams, or you will help others build theirs. Apply what you learn, or you will be paid to help others apply theirs.

---

[7] B Bloom, 'Bloom's Taxonomy of Learning', 1982.

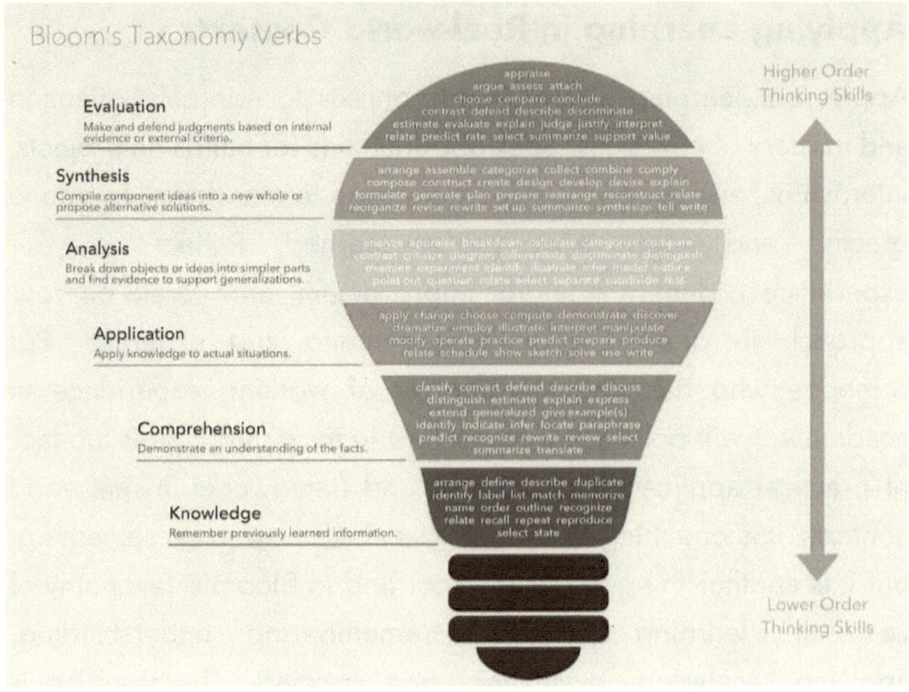

Bloom's taxonomy of learning[8]

Setting Learning Goals

Set specific learning goals to guide your continuous education and skill development efforts. Identify areas of knowledge or skills gaps relevant to your career aspirations and establish actionable steps to address them. Break down larger learning goals into smaller, achievable milestones and track your progress over time to stay motivated and focused. If you are not already registered for professional memberships relevant to your career, you should aim to do so immediately. They give you some level of credibility as a professional in that field and help you set learning goals through

---

[8] Nick Grantham, 'Bloom's Taxonomy Verbs - Free Chart and Handout- Fractus Learning', https://www.fractuslearning.com/, 25 January 2016, https://www.fractuslearning.com/blooms-taxonomy-verbs-free-chart/.

your CPD record of activities and forward plan for the next year. Some professional memberships also offer courses that can help you progress along your career path and provide a good pool of like-minded network professionals like yourself. Leverage these opportunities to see areas where you could improve and make the most of connections to ensure you are on the right path.

Summary

Embracing lifelong learning is essential for adapting to the dynamic nature of today's workforce and unlocking new opportunities for personal and professional growth. By cultivating a growth mindset, exploring diverse learning opportunities, seeking mentorship, building a personal learning network, applying learning in real-world contexts, and setting learning goals, you can stay ahead of the curve and thrive in your career journey. Commit to continuous learning as a lifelong pursuit and embrace the journey of growth, discovery, and transformation.

Career Mastery Exercise

The Need for Lifelong Learning

1. **Identify Key Skills:** List the key skills and knowledge areas relevant to your industry that require continuous development. Consider both technical and soft skills.
2. **Annual Learning Goal:** Commit to learning at least one new skill each year. Choose from certification courses, technical skills, soft skills, or management and leadership skills. Track your progress and reflect on how this new knowledge has benefited your career.

3. **CPD Log:** Start a Continuing Professional Development (CPD) log to record your learning activities and set goals for future learning. Review and update this log regularly to stay on track.

Embracing a Growth Mindset

1. **Growth Mindset Reflection:** Recall a time when you faced a significant challenge or failure. Reflect on how you overcame it and what you learned from the experience. Write down these reflections to remind yourself of your resilience.

2. **Challenge Yourself:** Identify an area in your career where you feel less confident. Set a goal to improve in this area by seeking out new challenges and learning opportunities.

3. **Feedback Loop:** Seek feedback from colleagues, mentors, or supervisors on your performance and areas for improvement. Use this feedback to set new learning goals and refine your approach.

Exploring Diverse Learning Opportunities

1. **Online Courses:** Research and enrol in an online course that interests you and aligns with your career goals. Platforms like Coursera, Udemy, and LinkedIn Learning offer a wide range of topics.

2. **Workshops and Seminars:** Attend at least one workshop, seminar, or webinar related to your field each quarter. Reflect on what you learned and how you can apply it to your work.

3. **Interdisciplinary Learning:** Explore courses or workshops outside your primary field to gain a broader perspective and develop transferable skills.

Seeking Mentorship and Guidance

1. **Find a Mentor:** Identify potential mentors within your network or industry. Reach out to them and express your interest in learning from their experiences and seeking their guidance.
2. **Mentorship Meetings:** Schedule regular meetings with your mentor to discuss your progress, challenges, and career goals. Prepare questions and topics in advance to make the most of these sessions.
3. **Peer Mentorship:** Consider becoming a mentor to someone else. Teaching and guiding others can reinforce your own knowledge and provide valuable insights.

Building a Personal Learning Network

1. **Professional Associations:** Join professional associations or organisations relevant to your field. Participate in their events, conferences, and networking opportunities.
2. **Online Communities:** Engage in online communities, forums, and social media groups related to your industry. Share resources, ask questions, and participate in discussions.
3. **Networking Events:** Attend at least one networking event each month. Connect with professionals who share your interests and goals, and exchange ideas and experiences.

Applying Learning in Real-world Contexts

1. **Hands-on Projects:** Seek out projects at work or in your personal time that allow you to apply new skills and knowledge. Reflect on your experiences and identify areas for improvement.
2. **Internships and Volunteering:** Consider internships or volunteer opportunities to gain practical experience in a new area. Use these experiences to build your portfolio and expand your skill set.
3. **Reflective Practice:** After completing a project or learning activity, take time to reflect on what you did well, what challenges you faced, and what you can do differently next time.

Setting Learning Goals

1. **Specific Goals:** Set specific learning goals for the next six months. Identify the skills or knowledge areas you want to improve and outline the steps you will take to achieve these goals.
2. **Achievable Milestones:** Break down your learning goals into smaller, achievable milestones. Set deadlines for each milestone and track your progress regularly.
3. **Professional Memberships:** Register for professional memberships relevant to your career. Use their resources and courses to guide your learning goals and CPD activities.

PRACTICAL EXPERIENCE

Gaining Hands-On Experience Through Internships, Projects, and Part-Time Jobs

Introduction

Practical experience is invaluable for bridging the gap between theory and practice, equipping you with the real-world skills and knowledge necessary for success in your chosen field. This section explores the importance of gaining hands-on experience through internships, projects, and part-time jobs and provides strategies for maximising the value of these opportunities.

> *"There is no job that is "too small" when you start; rather, you should go with a mindset to learn what you can while you are there, knowing very well that it is not your destination but just a beautiful chapter in your career story."*

Understanding the Value of Practical Experience

While academic knowledge lays the foundation for your career, practical experience provides the hands-on skills and insights needed to excel in the workplace. Internships, projects, and part-time jobs offer opportunities to apply classroom learning in real-world settings, gain industry-specific knowledge, and develop essential soft skills such as communication, teamwork, and problem-solving. As an international student from Nigeria who came for postgraduate studies in the UK in 2015, it was almost a massive shock to my system how much work experience mattered on this side of the world compared to the clime I was coming from. I was used to hearing first-class students get the best jobs straight out of school, and to be frank, internship opportunities in Nigeria were almost like a holiday where everything but actual work experience occurred. Like me, it was possible that you finished your degree in Nigeria as I did as a biochemistry student and barely ever operated a microscope. Our classrooms usually had over 300 students, and laboratory practical sessions were more, "Look at what I'm doing, and whenever you get a job, you can do the same." I knew I was somewhat unemployable after my first degree, as I did not know where to go. The fact that there were hardly any employment opportunities in Nigeria did not help, and you could see most graduates in white collar disciplines turning into entrepreneurs to make ends meet. This is a major reason why international students, mostly those from developing countries, struggle initially to land a good job until they have gained some level of work experience in the UK. The key thing to also point out here is that most Nigerians, speaking from experience, thrive abroad mainly because they have had that extensive theoretical knowledge but have been unable to apply it in real-world contexts to create something meaningful. However, the UK and other Western countries provide fertile ground for ideas to thrive and be cultivated into transformative, innovative solutions. I cannot overemphasise the importance of practical experience, as from Bloom's taxonomy, you can see the benefits for yourself as a professional and how you could gradually become an asset to an organisation you get involved with.

Securing Internship Opportunities

Internships are valuable for gaining practical experience and exploring potential career paths. Seek internship opportunities through career fairs, job boards, company websites, and networking events. Tailor your resume and cover letter to highlight relevant skills and experiences and prepare for interviews by researching the company and articulating your interest in the role. Most universities help students secure internship opportunities; however, these depend on how well you have performed as a student and your capability to apply what you have been taught to an industry context. Therefore, it is important to take your time searching for an internship position seriously by looking out for companies or organisations where you are sure to learn as much as possible. I had the opportunity of being an intern during my university days in Nigeria with Pipelines and Products Marketing Company Ltd, where I learned a lot about how the oil and gas industry works. While my first degree was in Biochemistry; I noticed there was some slight overlap between Environmental

Biochemistry and the oil and gas industry, e.g. bioremediation. Hence, I took up the challenge. However, it was fascinating to see that, in hindsight, my experience there shaped my career decision to study for a Master's in Petroleum and Environmental Technology. The rest is history, as you can see from previous sections in this book, where I have outlined how that has shaped my career to date.' Another thing to point out here is how a mother figure in my life, who was my boss during my internship, helped me turn my university grades around when I went back to school after the internship because she would always make time to go through my progress. That commitment from her motivated me to be serious when returning to school, as I had previously lost interest in school several times after changing courses. She reminded me of my intelligence as a child, and my lost confidence returned in massive folds. I had straight A's in my final year and went from a third class to second class upper, which enabled me to come to the UK for my Master's degree. From my story, I need not repeat that mentors are indispensable in this journey; you might find them during your internship.

Maximising Learning in Internships

During your internship, take the initiative to maximise your learning and contribution to the organisation. Seek opportunities to take on challenging projects, ask questions, and seek feedback from supervisors and colleagues. Demonstrate professionalism, reliability, and a willingness to learn, and showcase your skills and abilities through your work ethic and performance. Your character as a professional and your first work references are obtained from your internship period. It is important to note that internships are not holidays or time off school; they are the most critical time in your career journey because they are the first chance to sell yourself in the labour market. During my internship period, I was usually given weekly assignments and exercises by my boss to complete, which encouraged us to take stock of what we were learning and not just coasting along. Although I had some days where there was little to do in my department, my boss was so kind to let me experience other parts of the business, such as Operations, Finance, HR, Procurement, Maintenance, etc., which all added a wealth of experience to how businesses of that scale operate. I also had the opportunity to discuss my experiences with other interns, giving me a well-rounded understanding of operations in the oil and gas industry. Ensure that you make the most of your time during your internship, as doing so will put you in good stead for the future.

Undertaking Meaningful Projects

Engage in meaningful projects outside the classroom to gain practical experience and demonstrate your skills and abilities to potential employers. Volunteer for research projects, join student organisations or collaborate with peers on entrepreneurial ventures to develop your leadership, teamwork, and problem-solving skills. Showcase your project work in your resume, portfolio, or online profile to highlight your capabilities to employers. While I was going through some pictures which I took during my National Youth Service Corps (NYSC) days in Nigeria, I stumbled on some pictures which showed where I had volunteered as the Head of a

Health and Safety Workshop during which I demonstrated to all the thousands of corps members how to fight fires using fire extinguishers, fire blankets etc. Is it not funny how subconsciously, health and safety had been in my path all along? This is why I say that your vision must be driven by your passion and values, which is what will keep you going even when the days are not so bright. Anyway, engaging in these sorts of sensitisation and awareness projects gave me the practical experience of fighting fires, which, in fact, proved useful during my actual work experience.

Exploring Part-Time Jobs

Part-time jobs provide opportunities to gain practical experience, earn income, and develop transferable skills that are valuable in any career. Look for part-time jobs that align with your career interests and offer opportunities for skill development and growth. Retail, hospitality, customer service, and administrative roles are common part-time job options for students and young professionals. What part-time job did I not do when I first moved to the UK as a student except for care jobs? I did retail and hospitality jobs where I worked at football stadiums and horse racecourses, SIA door supervision at pubs and clubs, warehouse operative roles, handyman jobs, etc. While doing these jobs, I learned many soft skills such as communication, organisation, customer service, diplomacy and tact, conflict resolution, etc. There is no job that is "too small" when you start; rather, you should go with a mindset to learn what you can while you are there, knowing very well that it is not your destination, but just a beautiful chapter in your career story.

Balancing Work and Study

Balancing part-time work with academic studies requires effective time management, organisation, and prioritisation skills. Create a schedule that allows you to allocate time for work, study, and personal activities, and set realistic goals and deadlines to stay on track. Communicate with your employer and academic advisors to manage workload expectations and seek support when needed. For international students in the UK and other countries worldwide, ensure that you do not exceed the maximum working hours provided on your visas. Your priority during your studies is reflected in your title "student." You have already made huge financial commitments to study your chosen course, and it only makes sense that you channel most of your time toward your primary goal. However, the reality is that as a student, you also want to build work experience while getting some stipends on the side by way of a side hustle. Feel free to explore the various options available, but this should not come at a cost. My strategy was to dedicate a minimum of two hours a day, mostly immediately after classes, for my study in the library, which would include any assignments I had to complete. By doing so, I still had the rest of my day to catch up with friends and work. Amid all the chaos, remember to create a reward system (visiting friends, eating out, watching movies, etc.) for yourself so that you do not get drowned in the vicious cycle of study and work.

Reflecting on Experiences and Learning

Reflect on your practical experiences and learning to identify strengths, areas for improvement, and future career aspirations.

Keep a journal or portfolio to document your achievements, challenges, and lessons learned, and use reflection as a tool for personal and professional growth. Seek feedback from supervisors, mentors, and peers to gain insights into your performance and areas for development. One of the tools that has helped me improve consistently has been constructive feedback from my peers and mentors. However, it is important to have the ability to filter what is classified as constructive criticism vs destructive criticism, which focuses on just your problems without any solutions or forward. You should also make time to introspect and participate in self-reflection exercises where possible. I dare to say that every decision I have made in life that has ended well has not been taken by just myself. I have always sought the advice of experienced people who I know would give me an objective solution to my questions, rather than friends who might just say what you want to hear. Always pursue a life of reflection, as it is only when you look in the mirror that you can see the stains on your outfit.

Summary

Gaining hands-on experience through internships, projects, and part-time jobs is essential for building the skills, knowledge, and confidence needed to succeed in your career. Embrace these opportunities as valuable learning experiences and approach them with curiosity, enthusiasm, and a willingness to learn and grow. By taking initiative, maximising learning opportunities, and reflecting on your experiences, you can position yourself for success and unlock new opportunities for advancement and fulfilment in your career journey.

Career Mastery Exercise

Understanding the Value of Practical Experience

1. **Reflect on Past Experiences:** Write down any practical experiences you've had so far, such as internships, part-time jobs, or volunteer work. Reflect on the skills you gained and how they have contributed to your career development.
2. **Identify Skill Gaps:** List the skills and knowledge areas that you feel are lacking in your current skill set. Consider how gaining practical experience can help bridge these gaps.
3. **Set Learning Objectives:** Based on your identified skill gaps, set specific learning objectives for your next practical experience. Ensure these objectives are measurable and achievable.

Securing Internship Opportunities

1. **Research Companies:** Identify companies or organisations in your field of interest that offer internship opportunities. Use job boards, company websites, and networking events to find potential placements.
2. **Tailor Applications:** Customize your resume and cover letter for each internship application, highlighting relevant skills and experiences. Emphasise your enthusiasm and interest in the role.
3. **Prepare for Interviews:** Research the company and role thoroughly before interviews. Practise answering common interview questions and be ready to discuss how your skills and experiences make you a good fit.

Maximising Learning in Internships

1. **Proactive Engagement:** Take the initiative to seek out challenging projects and responsibilities during your internship. Show enthusiasm and a willingness to learn.
2. **Seek Feedback:** Regularly ask for feedback from your supervisors and colleagues. Use this feedback to improve your performance and develop your skills further.
3. **Network:** Build relationships with professionals in your organisation. Attend company events, join team meetings, and connect with colleagues on professional networking platforms like LinkedIn.

Undertaking Meaningful Projects

1. **Volunteer for Projects:** Look for opportunities to volunteer for projects within your university or community that align with your career interests. This can help you gain practical experience and demonstrate your commitment.
2. **Join Student Organisations:** Participate in student organisations related to your field. Take on leadership roles or collaborate on projects to develop your skills and expand your network.
3. **Showcase Your Work:** Create a portfolio or online profile to showcase your project work. Include details of the projects you have worked on, your contributions, and the outcomes achieved.

Exploring Part-Time Jobs

1. **Find Relevant Roles:** Search for part-time jobs that align with your career goals. Focus on roles that offer opportunities to develop relevant skills and gain industry experience.

2. **Transferable Skills:** Identify the transferable skills you can gain from part-time jobs, such as communication, teamwork, and problem-solving. Reflect on how these skills can benefit your career.

3. **Professionalism:** Approach part-time jobs with a professional attitude. Demonstrate reliability, a strong work ethic, and a willingness to learn, regardless of the role.

Balancing Work and Study

1. **Time Management:** Create a weekly schedule that balances your work, study, and personal commitments. Prioritise tasks and set realistic deadlines to manage your workload effectively.

2. **Study Routine:** Dedicate specific times each day to study and complete assignments. Use techniques such as the Pomodoro Technique to stay focused and productive.

3. **Seek Support:** Communicate with your employer and academic advisors about your commitments. Seek support if you feel overwhelmed and explore options for flexible working or study arrangements.

Reflecting on Experiences and Learning

1. **Keep a Journal:** Maintain a journal to document your practical experiences, achievements, challenges, and lessons learned. Reflect on your growth and identify areas for improvement.

2. **Seek Constructive Feedback:** Regularly ask for feedback from supervisors, mentors, and peers. Use this feedback to enhance your performance and develop your skills.

3. **Self-Reflection:** Set aside time for self-reflection to evaluate your progress towards your career goals. Adjust your plans and objectives based on your reflections and feedback.

NETWORKING

—◆—

*Cultivating Professional
Relationships and Mentors*

Introduction

Networking is more than exchanging business cards at events or connecting with people on social media. It is about building genuine relationships, fostering connections, and seeking mentorship that can propel your career forward. In this section, we will explore the importance of networking, strategies for cultivating professional relationships, and the value of mentorship in your career journey.

> *"Your network is your net worth."*
>
> **- Porter Gale**

The Power of Networking

Networking is a cornerstone of career development, providing opportunities for collaboration, learning, and growth. Whether attending industry conferences, joining professional associations, or engaging in online networking communities, your connections can open doors to new opportunities, insights, and perspectives. Networking allows you to expand your professional circle, tap into valuable resources, and stay informed about industry trends and developments. My current job role was purely a function of networking. My previous line manager asked me to represent the team in a Health and Safety Away Day organised somewhere in Central London. This is an event where all health and safety representatives from every department in the organisation come together to network with one another and proffer solutions to any pertinent issues while sharing insights on relevant health and safety data. During the session, my current line manager (he was not at the time) was employed by the organisation as the Lead Human Factors Specialist, and he delivered a presentation on human factors. After the event, I approached him and had a long discussion with him about human factors, which, in fact, was my major domain during my MSc and PhD programmes. We exchanged details afterwards, and he informed me that the organisation was in dire need of a Human Factors Specialist, and he saw me as the perfect fit. I applied for the role, and the rest is history. We have maintained an amazing working relationship ever since. Networking is an invaluable component of career development. As Porter Gale's popular saying goes, "Your network is your net worth."[9]

---

[9] Porter Gale, *Your Network Is Your Net Worth: Unlock the Hidden Power of Connections for Wealth, Success, and Happiness in the Digital Age* (Simon and Schuster, 2013).

Strategies for Effective Networking

Effective networking is about building authentic connections and nurturing relationships over time. Start by identifying your networking goals and target audience. Be proactive in contacting individuals who share your interests or work in your industry. Attend networking events, conferences, and workshops where you can meet like-minded professionals and engage in meaningful conversations. Listen actively, ask insightful questions, and demonstrate genuine interest in others' experiences and perspectives. Follow up with contacts after networking events and stay in touch regularly to maintain and strengthen your connections. Returning to my interaction with my current line manager after the Health and Safety Away Day, we maintained contact afterwards. We stayed connected with industry trends while sharing insights on how our organisation could benefit from the revolutionary innovations within the sector. Bear in mind that we were not yet working together at this time, but there was a genuine connection between us as career professionals in a field where not many experts exist currently. In fact, my line manager always asserts that "Human Factors professionals are as scarce as brain surgeons," and I tend to agree with him. This is a novel field that only started gaining traction after the second world war, when the United States lost hundreds of planes in accidents deemed 'pilot error;' however, design flaws were discovered, which also led to the development of human factors as a discipline. In essence, I am reiterating that you should go beyond just your personal aggrandisement to establish and build a genuine relationship with your networks, as this will smoothen your path when you need assistance in your career journey.

The Value of Mentorship

Mentorship is a powerful tool for personal and professional growth, providing guidance, support, and encouragement from experienced professionals who have walked the path before you. A mentor can offer valuable insights, advice, and feedback, helping you navigate challenges, make informed decisions, and accelerate your career progression. Seek out mentors who have expertise in your field, share your values, and are willing to invest their time and energy in your development. Be proactive in seeking mentorship opportunities and cultivate relationships based on mutual respect, trust, and shared goals. I have been fortunate to have valuable mentors in my life, especially regarding my career. I have mentors I met during my education who made me discover health and safety as a career and who have stayed connected to date to monitor my progress. Like I said earlier, most of the courses I have taken that have propelled me in my career have been recommended by mentors. I also pointed out how my previous line manager always put me in the front of opportunities, which then allowed me to network with my current line manager and land my current role. Furthermore, I became a Chartered Human Factors Specialist and Ergonomist based on a recommendation from my current line manager, who advised that from our discussions, he can attest that I am more than qualified for it. However, I did not realise this until I started filling out my portfolio of evidence to submit to the awarding body. It was only then I had the opportunity to take stock of all I had done, and it was an eye-opening moment. Remember, I have spoken and will speak more about the power of reflection in your career journey, as this is a practice you must embrace to get to the top. Talking of mentorship, it was a requirement before you attained that Chartership that you must have a mentor who is already Chartered. My line manager, as well as two of my health and safety mentors, were more than happy to stand in for me as referees, and that was, in a nutshell, how mentorship helped me navigate that pivotal point in my career.

Building Reciprocal Relationships

Networking is a two-way street; building reciprocal relationships is key to long-term success. Be generous with your time, knowledge, and resources, and offer support and assistance to others whenever possible. Share your expertise, connections, and insights with your network, and be willing to lend a helping hand to those in need. Building a reputation as a valuable and trusted resource within your network can lead to new opportunities, referrals, and collaborations down the line. I am someone who genuinely cherishes my connections and relationships, whether family, social, work, business, or life related. My ideology is that in a mutual relationship with a second party, if one person keeps pouring into it without that gesture being reciprocated, it is only a matter of time before that person gets drained and has nothing more to give. To keep that energy in the relationship thriving, efforts are required on both ends to keep pouring themselves into nurturing the relationship. This might be just by randomly checking in to see how they are faring personally and professionally, arranging a meet-up, sending relevant information to each other that could help the other person, etc. As a Christian, I also pray for my connections and networks because I believe that if all is well with them, it will be well with me and vice versa, especially if the relationship is genuine. If my line manager, spouse, colleague, friend, or family is groggy, it will inadvertently affect me and could deter my entire day. So, in the same vein, building reciprocal relationships with your network is healthy and helpful.

Navigating Networking Challenges

Networking can sometimes feel daunting or intimidating, especially for introverted or shy individuals. Remember that networking is a skill that can be developed over time, and it is okay to start small and gradually build your confidence. Focus on quality over quantity when it comes to networking and prioritise building genuine connections with individuals who align with your values and goals. Do not be afraid to step out of your comfort zone and attend networking events or engage in online communities where you can meet new people and expand your network. Did I tell you that I am somewhat of an introvert? Oh yes, I am, and it might be difficult to spot if you have consciously read this book to this point. At a point, I dared not stand before people to say anything because I would just freeze. Even to date, there are times when I do have social anxiety and do not want to be around people, and that is fine. However, it is wrong to remain in that space for a long time (as humans are social animals) because what happens is that the longer you stay there, the more you drain your self-confidence and begin to develop resentment for everyone, including those who have never done anything wrong to you. One thing that helped me beat this challenge was joining a church choir in 2006, which made me start coming out of my shell. It does not all happen in one day, but you will get used to being comfortable in certain circles over time. See why I said certain circles, because you cannot be comfortable with everyone, and again, that is fine. Take time to analyse your relationships and see how you click with each person, and that will make you understand, not just through your personality but theirs as well, how to manage those relationships exclusively.

Summary

Networking is a fundamental aspect of career development, providing opportunities for growth, learning, and collaboration. By cultivating genuine relationships, seeking mentorship, and nurturing your network over time, you can unlock new opportunities, expand your horizons, and achieve greater success in your chosen field. Embrace networking as a strategic tool for career advancement and invest in building meaningful connections that will support and empower you on your journey to mastery.

Career Mastery Exercise

The Power of Networking

1. **Reflect on Current Network:** List the key people in your current professional network. Identify the connections that have positively impacted your career and those you would like to strengthen.
2. **Expand Your Network:** Set a goal to attend at least one industry conference, professional association meeting, or online networking event each month.
3. **Follow Up:** After each event, follow up with new connections via email or LinkedIn. Personalise your message, referencing something specific from your conversation to reinforce the connection.

Strategies for Effective Networking

1. **Set Networking Goals:** Define what you want to achieve through networking, whether it's finding a mentor, learning about new opportunities, or gaining industry insights.

2. **Active Listening:** Practise active listening during networking events. Show genuine interest in others' experiences by asking open-ended questions and providing thoughtful responses.

3. **Regular Check-ins:** Schedule regular check-ins with your key connections. This could be a quick coffee, a catch-up call, or a simple message to maintain and strengthen your relationship.

The Value of Mentorship

1. **Identify Potential Mentors:** Look for individuals in your industry who have the experience and values that resonate with you. Reach out to them, expressing your admiration for their work and your interest in mentorship.

2. **Set Clear Expectations:** Once you have a mentor, set clear expectations for the relationship. Discuss your career goals, preferred methods of communication, and how often you would like to meet.

3. **Be a Good Mentee:** Be proactive in seeking advice and feedback. Show appreciation for your mentor's time and insights by implementing their advice and updating them on your progress.

Building Reciprocal Relationships

1. **Offer Help:** Be generous with your time and expertise. Offer to help your network connections with their projects or challenges.
2. **Share Resources:** Regularly share valuable articles, books, or contacts with your network. This shows you are invested in their success as well.
3. **Celebrate Successes:** Acknowledge and celebrate the successes of your network. Send congratulatory messages for achievements and milestones.

Navigating Networking Challenges

1. **Start Small:** If large networking events are intimidating, start with smaller, more manageable gatherings or one-on-one meetings.
2. **Practise Your Introduction:** Prepare a brief, engaging introduction about yourself. Practise it until you feel confident delivering it naturally.
3. **Leverage Online Platforms:** Use online platforms like LinkedIn to connect with professionals in your field. Participate in relevant groups and discussions to build your presence and confidence.

CHAPTER

THREE

DEVELOPING EXPERTISE

SPECIALISATION

— . —

Choosing Your Niche and
Becoming an Expert in Your Field

Introduction

In a world where knowledge is abundant, and competition is fierce, specialisation is the key to standing out and excelling in your chosen field. This section explores the importance of choosing a niche and becoming an expert and provides strategies for achieving mastery and recognition in your area of specialisation.

"True dominance and influence come from when you are the first person that crosses people's minds when they think about your sector."

- Dr. Myles Munroe

Understanding the Power of Specialisation

Specialisation involves focusing your efforts and expertise on a specific niche or area within your field. By narrowing your focus, you can deepen your knowledge, hone your skills, and differentiate yourself from competitors. Specialisation allows you to become known as an expert in your niche, attracting collaboration, recognition, and advancement opportunities. We all know the saying, "Jack of all trades, master of none." Well, that same principle applies when we talk about career development. I learnt from how the educational system is structured that the higher you go, the more specialised you become in a certain field. For example, when I started primary school (and I believe the same applies to most people), I learned all the subjects, whether arts, science, social science, etc. In secondary school, you are split into either science or art classes, where you start developing a flair for your chosen career path based on how well you excel in certain subjects or where you effortlessly can express yourself. Before you get into university, you must decide on the ultimate path you want to take, which will guide you to your first degree. Your master's degree then specialises in a subject area in that field of study, while your PhD then focuses on a particular topic within the subject area of that field of study. You can clearly see how that triangle of specialisation shapes as you climb higher up the ladder. However, this does not in any way stop you from branching out and doing gaining specialty in other disciplines. After all, most people do not realise that the full version of the quote I mentioned earlier states, "A jack of all trades is a master of none, but oftentimes better than a master of one." One thing I will advise here is ensure that you fill one cup before pouring into another.

Identifying Your Niche

Start by identifying your passions, strengths, and interests within your field. Reflect on the aspects of your work that energise and inspire you, and consider the unique skills or experiences that set you apart from others. Conduct research to identify emerging trends, gaps in the market, and areas of opportunity that align with your expertise and aspirations. In all honesty, identifying my niche was a little bit of a struggle because sometimes, you can be so good in everything that it now becomes confusing in what you should specialise. However, this is where mentorship and guidance could prove valuable. Also, schools' Guidance and Counselling teams should endeavour to help students identify their niches by having career fairs and one-to-one sessions with them. On the other hand, I must clearly state this controversial opinion from my experience: your passion does not always have to align with your career path. Or let me paraphrase a little bit. What you love to do might not be what puts food on the table. You must not do what you love but love what you do. One of my favourite life quotes, which I got from my mother, is, "Whatever is worth doing is worth doing well." This quote was from a Bible verse by the wisest man to ever live, King Solomon.

> **"** *"Whatever you do, do well. For when you go to the grave, there will be no work or planning or knowledge or wisdom."*
>
> **Ecclesiastes 9:10 NLT**[10] **"**

---

[10] Holy Bible, 'New Living Translation', *Gift and Award Edition*, 1996.

Choosing Your Specialisation

Once you have identified potential niches, evaluate them based on factors such as market demand, growth potential, and personal fit. Consider the level of competition, the availability of resources and support, and the alignment with your long-term goals and values. Choose a specialisation that aligns with your passions, leverages your strengths, and offers opportunities for growth and fulfilment. Now, remember I said you must not always do what you love. One of the reasons for that is when you start your career, you might have to do certain courses or jobs that you are not passionate about. However, you must love these jobs because they are not the destination but a route to your goal. I have discussed embracing your journey and will speak more about it, but it is important. You cannot get back anytime you feel sorry for yourself, but you can make the most of your time wherever you find yourself. Easier said than done, as I personally have fallen severally into that vicious cycle of always wanting more and not appreciating the journey. However, when you love what you do, over time, you will then have the means to fuel what you love, your passion. The money you get from doing your jobs can be the stepping stone that can afford you the capital to open that business, start that craft, launch that brand, etc. However, be careful to focus on passion and what the world is telling you. Is your passion profitable, or is your passion even your strength? If not, then develop yourself in the area you are passionate about.

Becoming an Expert

Becoming an expert in your chosen niche requires dedication, perseverance, and continuous learning. Immerse yourself in your niche by reading books, attending conferences, and participating in online forums and communities. Seek mentorship and guidance from established experts in your field and learn from their experiences and insights. I will say that one thing that helped me gain expertise in my field was undertaking my PhD programme. During this time, I researched thousands of journal papers from established authorities in my field, which helped me develop my own framework and model for the oil and gas industry. A key aspect of the PhD research process was that some of my data had to be collected from professionals in the oil and gas industry, which gave reliability and validity to the study findings. I am also helping my organisation develop a similar framework and model for the UK bio sector from this study. From my experience, it is evident that gradually building your competence (knowledge, ability, training, and experience) from established authorities in your field is key to mastering your career and becoming a recognised authority in your area of specialisation.

Building Your Reputation

Establishing yourself as an expert requires building a strong personal brand and reputation within your niche. Share your knowledge and expertise through blog posts, articles, presentations, and social media platforms. Contribute to industry publications, speak at conferences, and participate in professional networking events to raise your visibility and credibility. As part of my career development within my niche, I started publishing journal articles in reputable databases related to my field, such as ScienceDirect, Scopus, Wiley Online Library, Taylor, and Francis. By doing so, I gained much traction and became popular among other professionals within my field's academic and industrial sectors. A major fact to note is that when you start contributing to knowledge either by writing, speaking, implementing, or influencing, true mastery stems. You find true fulfilment in what you do when you realise the impact it has beyond the scope of your sector and the world at large, and this can only be done when you put yourself out there. You may face imposter syndrome when you feel you are not good enough, but this is normal, especially when you have set high standards and targets for yourself. If your dream does not scare you, it is not big enough. Ensure you thoroughly immerse yourself in your niche to give you the much-needed competence to feel confident when speaking to someone about your career.

Delivering Exceptional Value

Focus on delivering exceptional value to your audience by solving their problems, addressing their needs, and providing innovative solutions. Stay current with industry trends, best practices, and emerging technologies to maintain relevance and competitiveness in your niche. Continuously seek client, colleague, and mentor feedback to refine your offerings and enhance your expertise. One good way I have implemented this in my career is by attending conferences and workshops and watching videos on YouTube about any aspects of my field I need to develop more competence.

I also request anonymous feedback from colleagues at work to help me highlight my strengths and weaknesses, which will assist me in creating a personal development plan. Certifications are also relevant in some rapidly evolving sectors, such as IT, where there are emerging technologies consistently, and you need to keep yourself updated, or else you risk getting left behind by your contemporaries.

Expanding Your Influence

As you gain expertise and recognition in your niche, look for opportunities to expand your influence and impact within your industry. Collaborate with other experts, contribute to collaborative projects and initiatives, and mentor aspiring professionals to share your knowledge and insights. Be generous with your expertise and support, and strive to make a positive difference in your field. No man is an island, as the saying goes. For instance, in the process of expanding my influence and impact in my industry sector, I have collaborated with various industry professionals on various projects around my health and safety consultancy company, Nancheez Ltd. As a matter of fact, one strategy I learnt was to arrange meetings with fellow experts in your field, including businesses that are your direct competition. This enables you both to benchmark each other, but more importantly, there might be services that one offers that the other does not. But, by working together, you both can produce referral packages for clients who want both services, and you both win. Have you ever wondered if McDonald's and KFC, for example, have their own niches of meals they make and stick purely to that? When you think of a Big Mac, you think of McDonalds. When you think of Southern fried chicken, you think of KFC.

Paraphrasing from the words of the late Myles Munroe, "True dominance and influence comes from when you are the first person that crosses people's minds when they think about your sector."[11]

Summary

Specialisation is the pathway to becoming a recognised authority and leader in your field. By choosing a niche that aligns with your passions and expertise, committing to continuous learning and improvement, and delivering exceptional value to your audience, you can achieve mastery and recognition as an expert in your chosen specialisation. Embrace the journey of specialisation to unlock your full potential and make a lasting impact in your industry.

Career Mastery Exercise

Understanding the Power of Specialisation

1. **Reflect on Your Journey:** Write down your academic and career journey so far. Identify the areas where you have excelled and the subjects or tasks that you have enjoyed the most.

2. **List Your Skills:** Create a list of your top skills and areas of expertise. Highlight those that are most relevant to your current job or desired career path.

3. **Identify Knowledge Gaps:** Assess your current knowledge and skills to identify any gaps that need to be filled to become an expert in your chosen niche.

---

[11] Myles Munroe, *The Principle and Power of Kingdom Citizenship: Keys to Experiencing Heaven on Earth* (Destiny Image Publishers, 2016).

Identifying Your Niche

1. **Passion and Strengths:** Reflect on what excites you most in your field. Make a list of your passions, strengths, and interests.
2. **Market Research:** Conduct research to identify emerging trends, gaps in the market, and areas of high demand. Look for opportunities that align with your strengths and passions.
3. **Consult a Mentor:** Discuss your findings with a mentor or career advisor to gain their perspective on your potential niches and seek their guidance on narrowing down your options.

Choosing Your Specialisation

1. **Evaluate Niches:** Compare the potential niches you have identified. Consider factors such as market demand, growth potential, competition, and personal fit.
2. **Long-Term Goals:** Reflect on how each niche aligns with your long-term career goals and values. Choose the one that offers the most potential for growth and fulfilment.
3. **Create an Action Plan:** Develop a detailed action plan outlining the steps you need to take to establish yourself in your chosen niche.

Becoming an Expert

1. **Continuous Learning:** Commit to continuous learning by reading books, attending conferences, and participating in online courses related to your niche.
2. **Seek Mentorship:** Identify and reach out to established experts in your field for mentorship. Learn from their

experiences and seek their guidance to enhance your knowledge and skills.

3. **Practical Experience:** Look for opportunities to apply your knowledge in real-world settings. This could include projects at work, volunteering, or freelance work in your niche.

Building Your Reputation

1. **Content Creation:** Share your knowledge and expertise through blog posts, articles, and social media. Establish a strong online presence to raise your visibility and credibility.

2. **Public Speaking:** Seek opportunities to speak at industry conferences, webinars, and workshops. Sharing your insights and experiences will help establish you as a thought leader in your niche.

3. **Networking:** Build relationships with other professionals in your field. Attend industry events, join professional associations, and engage in online communities to expand your network.

Delivering Exceptional Value

1. **Client Feedback:** Regularly seek feedback from clients, colleagues, and mentors. Use this feedback to refine your services and offerings.

2. **Stay Current:** Keep up-to-date with industry trends, best practices, and emerging technologies. Ensure your knowledge and skills remain relevant and competitive.

3. **Innovative Solutions:** Focus on delivering innovative solutions that address your audience's needs and problems. Strive to exceed expectations and add significant value through your work.

Expanding Your Influence

1. **Collaborative Projects:** Collaborate with other experts on projects and initiatives. This can lead to new opportunities, referrals, and increased recognition in your field.
2. **Mentor Others:** Share your knowledge and experiences by mentoring aspiring professionals. Helping others can reinforce your expertise and expand your influence.
3. **Publications and Media:** Contribute to industry publications, podcasts, and media outlets. Sharing your insights with a broader audience can enhance your reputation and reach.

MASTERY THROUGH PRACTICE

— ⋄ —

*Deliberate Practice Techniques
and Habit Formation*

Introduction

Mastery in any field is not merely a product of talent or luck but the result of deliberate and disciplined practice. In this section, we will explore the concept of deliberate practice and how habit formation plays a crucial role in achieving mastery in your chosen craft.

"

"I fear not the man who has practised 10,000 kicks once, but I fear the man who has practised one kick 10,000 times"

- Bruce Lee

"

Understanding Deliberate Practice

Deliberate practice is a systematic and purposeful approach to skill development that focuses on pushing beyond one's comfort zone, identifying weaknesses, and targeting specific areas for improvement. Unlike mindless repetition, deliberate practice involves breaking down complex skills into manageable components, seeking feedback, and engaging in focused, structured practice sessions to continuously improve. For those familiar with how a PhD programme is structured, part of the requirements to progress to the next year is to break down your thesis into deliverables, which will be assessed annually by a Progress Review Panel. This helps the researcher understand what is required of them at each stage and develop a plan to achieve each of these "mini targets." My university organises a competition called "Visualise your thesis," which involves presenting an overview of your thesis in 60 seconds to a non-specialist audience. This helps the researcher sometimes introspect and see how well they understand the requirements and benefits of their work and how well they can articulate that to someone with no experience of what it entails. Similarly, this sort of deliberate practice can be useful not just for academics but for industry professionals as well.

> **"**
>
> *"Discipline and consistency define the distance between the life you have and the life you want."*
>
> **- Vusi Thembekwayo[12]**
>
> **"**

---

[12] Vusi Thembekwayo, *Business & Life Lessons from a Black Dragon* (Tafelberg, 2018).

Key Principles of Deliberate Practice

- **Specific Goals:** Set clear and specific goals for each practice session, focusing on areas that require improvement.
- **Focus and Concentration:** Maintain high levels of concentration and focus during practice to maximise learning and skill acquisition.
- **Feedback and Reflection:** Seek feedback from mentors, coaches, or peers, and reflect on your performance to identify areas for growth and refinement.
- **Repetition and Iteration:** Repeat practice drills and exercises consistently, gradually increasing difficulty and complexity over time.
- **Patience and Persistence:** Embrace the process of mastery with patience and persistence, understanding that progress may be slow but steady.

Deliberate Practice Techniques

- **Chunking:** Break down complex skills or tasks into smaller, more manageable chunks to facilitate learning and mastery.
- **Visualisation:** Mentally rehearse and visualise successful execution of skills or tasks to enhance performance and confidence.
- **Slow Practice:** Slow down the practice tempo to focus on precision, technique, and control, gradually increasing speed as proficiency improves.
- **Spaced Repetition:** Distribute practice sessions over time, spacing them out for maximum retention and long-term skill development.

- **Interleaved Practice:** Mix and vary practice drills and exercises to challenge adaptability and promote deeper learning and skill transfer.

Forming Habits for Mastery

Habit formation is essential for sustaining long-term practice and achieving mastery in your craft. You can create an environment that fosters continuous learning and growth by establishing consistent routines and rituals. Start by identifying specific behaviours or actions that support your goals and incorporate them into your daily or weekly schedule. Over time, these behaviours will become ingrained habits that require less effort and conscious effort to maintain. There was a myth that it takes twenty-one days to form a habit if an activity is done consistently over that period. However, according to a European Journal of Social Psychology study, forming a habit takes from eighteen to two hundred and fifty-four days, averaging about sixty-six days.[13] It was also discovered that even if the behaviour was skipped once during that time, it did not have a massive impact on habit formation if people returned to that activity immediately. I remember waking up at 5am every morning for six years in secondary school to prepare for the day. After secondary school, I always woke up at 5am, even when I had nothing to do. The same applies to forming habits that can help you achieve your set goals by doing it over time. As the saying goes, "practice makes perfect."

---

[13] Phillippa Lally et al., 'How Are Habits Formed: Modelling Habit Formation in the Real World', *European Journal of Social Psychology* 40, no. 6 (1 October 2010): 998–1009, https://doi.org/10.1002/ejsp.674.

Strategies for Habit Formation

- **Start Small:** Establish small, manageable habits that are easy to implement and sustain.
- **Consistency:** Commit to practising your habits consistently, regardless of external circumstances or obstacles.
- **Accountability:** Hold yourself accountable for sticking to your habits by tracking your progress, setting reminders, or sharing your goals with others.
- **Flexibility:** Be adaptable and willing to adjust your habits as needed to accommodate changes in your schedule or circumstances.
- **Rewards and Reinforcement:** Celebrate your successes and milestones along the way and reward yourself for sticking to your habits to reinforce positive behaviour.

Summary

Mastery through practice is a continuous growth and improvement journey that requires dedication, discipline, and perseverance. By embracing deliberate practice techniques and forming habits supporting your goals, you can unlock your full potential and master your chosen craft. Commit to the process with patience and persistence, and trust that every practice session brings you one step closer to excellence.

Career Mastery Exercise

Understanding Deliberate Practice

1. **Set Clear Goals:** Define specific goals for each practice session. Focus on areas that need improvement rather than simply practising what you already excel at.
   - Example: If you are a musician, aim to master a particular piece or technique that challenges you.
2. **Create a Practice Plan:** Develop a structured plan for your practice sessions. Allocate time for warm-ups, focused practice on specific skills, and cool-downs.
   - Example: Divide a one-hour practice session into 15 minutes of warm-up, 30 minutes of focused practice, and 15 minutes of reviewing progress.
3. **Seek Feedback:** Regularly ask for feedback from mentors, coaches, or peers. Reflect on their input to identify strengths and areas for improvement.
   - Example: Record your practice sessions and review them with a mentor to gain constructive feedback.

Key Principles of Deliberate Practice

1. **Specific Goals:** Set clear, specific, and measurable goals for each practice session.
   - Exercise: Write down three specific goals you want to achieve in your next practice session.

2. **Focus and Concentration:** Eliminate distractions and maintain high levels of concentration during practice.
   - Exercise: Create a dedicated practice space that is free from distractions and conducive to focused practice.

3. **Feedback and Reflection:** Regularly seek feedback and take time to reflect on your performance.
   - o Exercise: Keep a practice journal where you note feedback received, personal reflections, and areas for improvement.

4. **Repetition and Iteration:** Consistently repeat practice drills and gradually increase their difficulty.
   - o Exercise: Identify a challenging skill and commit to practising it daily for a month, gradually increasing its complexity.

5. **Patience and Persistence:** Embrace the slow and steady process of mastery.
   - o Exercise: Reflect on a time when patience and persistence paid off in your practice. Write down what you learned from that experience.

Deliberate Practice Techniques

1. **Chunking:** Break down complex tasks into smaller, manageable parts.
   - o Exercise: Choose a complex skill and break it down into five smaller components. Practise each component individually.

2. **Visualisation:** Mentally rehearse successful execution of skills.
   - o Exercise: Spend 10 minutes each day visualising yourself performing a skill perfectly before physically practising it.

3. **Slow Practice:** Slow down your practice tempo to focus on precision and technique.
   - o Exercise: Practise a skill at half-speed, paying close attention to accuracy and form. Gradually increase the speed as you improve.

4. **Spaced Repetition:** Space out your practice sessions for maximum retention.
   - o Exercise: Create a practice schedule that includes spaced intervals (e.g., practise a skill on Mondays, Wednesdays, and Fridays).

5. **Interleaved Practice:** Mix different types of practice drills to enhance adaptability.
   - o Exercise: Design a practice session that includes a variety of skills and drills, mixing them up to challenge your adaptability.

Forming Habits for Mastery

1. **Start Small:** Begin with small, manageable habits that are easy to implement.
   - o Exercise: Identify a small habit that supports your practice goals, such as practising for 10 minutes daily, and commit to it for a week.

2. **Consistency:** Practise your habits consistently to build momentum.
   - o Exercise: Use a habit tracker to mark each day you successfully complete your practice habit.

3. **Accountability:** Hold yourself accountable by tracking your progress or sharing your goals with someone.
   - Exercise: Share your practice goals with a friend or mentor and provide them with regular updates on your progress.

4. **Flexibility:** Be willing to adjust your habits to fit changes in your schedule.
   - Exercise: Create a flexible practice plan that can be adapted to different circumstances, such as shorter sessions on busy days.

5. **Rewards and Reinforcement:** Celebrate your achievements and reward yourself for sticking to your habits.
   - Exercise: Set up a reward system for yourself. For example, treat yourself to something enjoyable after completing a week of consistent practice.

SEEKING FEEDBACK

— · —

Embracing Constructive Criticism
and Iterative Improvement

Introduction

Feedback is a powerful tool for growth and development, providing valuable insights into our strengths, weaknesses, and areas for improvement. In this section, we will explore the importance of seeking feedback, embracing constructive criticism, and leveraging it to catalyse improvement in personal and professional pursuits.

> *"You need to have the ability to differentiate between constructive and destructive criticism, of which the latter focuses on just problems and not solutions."*

Understanding the Value of Feedback

Feedback serves as a mirror that reflects our performance, illuminating blind spots and offering guidance for growth. Whether from mentors, peers, or supervisors, feedback provides perspectives and insights that we may not be able to see on our own. Embracing feedback as a gift rather than criticism is essential for unlocking our full potential and achieving excellence. If you remember the role of mentors and how they can shorten your career journey, a large part of that comes through feedback. For example, if you go on the wrong path and stop asking someone for directions, you can navigate to the right path and continue your journey. However, if you have a closed mindset and feel like you do not require help, you might just be headed for a dead-end and have to take the painful turn back to retrace your steps. Implementing actions from the feedback I received during my coursework assignments, internship in Nigeria, thesis submissions, job assessments by my line manager, etc., all made me the professional I am today. Have I ever received feedback that was not constructive and just super critical for the sake of it? Yes. However, you need to be able to filter out what constructive and destructive criticism is, which focuses on just problems and not solutions.

Types of Feedback

- **Positive Feedback:** Acknowledges strengths, achievements, and successes, reinforcing positive behaviour and encouraging continued progress.

- **Constructive Criticism:** Identifies areas for improvement, offering specific, actionable suggestions for growth and development.
- **Developmental Feedback:** Focuses on skill-building and professional growth, providing guidance and support to help individuals reach their full potential.

Seeking Feedback Effectively

- **Be Proactive:** Take the initiative to seek feedback from mentors, colleagues, and stakeholders rather than waiting for it to be offered.
- **Ask Specific Questions:** Request feedback on specific aspects of your performance or behaviour to elicit targeted, actionable responses.
- **Create a Safe Environment:** Foster open, honest communication and create a safe space for feedback by welcoming diverse perspectives and constructive criticism.
- **Listen Actively:** Listen attentively to feedback without becoming defensive or dismissive and ask clarifying questions to ensure understanding.
- **Express Gratitude:** Appreciate and acknowledge your feedback, expressing gratitude for the insights and perspectives shared.

Embracing Constructive Criticism

- **Separate the Feedback from the Person:** Focus on the content of the feedback rather than the delivery or the person providing it.

- **Reframe Criticism as Opportunity:** View constructive criticism as an opportunity for growth and improvement rather than a personal attack or failure.
- **Embrace a Growth Mindset:** Adopt a growth mindset that sees challenges and setbacks as opportunities for learning and development.
- **Use Feedback to Inform Action:** Translate feedback into actionable steps for improvement, setting goals and implementing strategies to address areas of weakness.

Iterative Improvement

- **Continuous Improvement:** Embrace a continuous improvement mindset, seeking feedback regularly and making incremental changes over time.
- **Reflect and Iterate:** Reflect on past experiences and feedback to identify patterns and trends and iterate on your approach to achieve better outcomes.
- **Monitor Progress:** Track your progress over time and evaluate the effectiveness of your efforts, adjusting your strategies as needed to stay on course.

Summary

Seeking feedback is a powerful tool for growth and development, providing valuable insights and guidance for improvement. By embracing constructive criticism, soliciting diverse perspectives, and leveraging feedback as a catalyst for iterative improvement, you can unlock your full potential and achieve excellence in personal and professional endeavours. Embrace feedback as a gift that propels you forward on your journey of growth and mastery.

Career Mastery Exercise

Understanding the Value of Feedback

1. **Reflect on Past Feedback:** Think about a time when feedback significantly impacted your growth. What was the feedback, and how did it help you improve?
   - Exercise: Write a brief reflection on a specific instance where feedback led to a positive change in your personal or professional life.

2. **Feedback Journal:** Start a feedback journal to record the feedback you receive. Note the source, content, and your reflections on how to use it for growth.
   - Exercise: After each significant feedback session, write down the feedback and create an action plan to address the points raised.

Types of Feedback

1. **Identify Feedback Types:** Recognise the different types of feedback you receive and categorise them.
   - Exercise: Make a table with three columns—Positive Feedback, Constructive Criticism, and Developmental Feedback. Fill it with examples from your recent experiences.

2. **Seek Balanced Feedback:** Ensure you are receiving a balanced mix of feedback types to support your growth comprehensively.
   - Exercise: List the people in your network who can provide each type of feedback and plan to seek their input regularly.

Seeking Feedback Effectively

1. **Be Proactive:** Schedule regular feedback sessions with mentors, colleagues, or supervisors.
   - Exercise: Set a calendar reminder to request feedback every month from at least one person in your professional network.

2. **Ask Specific Questions:** Prepare targeted questions that focus on specific aspects of your performance or projects.
   - Exercise: Develop a list of five specific questions to ask during your next feedback session.

3. **Create a Safe Environment:** Foster an environment where feedback is encouraged and appreciated.
   - Exercise: During team meetings, openly invite feedback and ensure you acknowledge and thank contributors for their insights.

Embracing Constructive Criticism

1. **Separate Feedback from the Person:** Focus on the content rather than the delivery or the person giving it.
   - Exercise: When receiving feedback, take notes on the points raised without immediately reacting. Review these notes later to determine actionable steps.

2. **Reframe Criticism as Opportunity:** View constructive criticism as a chance to learn and grow.
   - Exercise: List three recent pieces of constructive criticism you received. Next to each, write down how you can use this feedback to improve.

3. **Embrace a Growth Mindset:** See challenges as opportunities for development.
   - o Exercise: Read Carol Dweck's book "Mindset: The New Psychology of Success" to deepen your understanding of growth mindset principles.

Iterative Improvement

1. **Continuous Improvement:** Regularly seek feedback and make incremental changes.
   - o Exercise: Implement a Plan-Do-Check-Act (PDCA) cycle for continuous improvement in a specific area of your work or personal life.

2. **Reflect and Iterate:** Reflect on feedback and adjust your approach accordingly.
   - o Exercise: After completing a project, review the feedback received and write down what you would do differently next time.

3. **Monitor Progress:** Track your progress and evaluate the effectiveness of your efforts.
   - o Exercise: Use a tool like a progress tracker or spreadsheet to monitor improvements over time, adjusting your strategies as necessary.

FOUR

OVERCOMING CHALLENGES

FAILURE AS A STEPPING STONE

Learning from Setbacks and Resilience Building

Introduction

Failure is an inevitable part of the journey towards success, but how we respond to setbacks ultimately determines our trajectory. In this section, we will explore the concept of failure as a stepping stone, learning from setbacks, and building resilience in the face of adversity.

> *"Humans were made to face challenges and sometimes fail, as failure is part of the plan and process of becoming. It is important to see success and failure as experiences rather than outcomes."*

Understanding Failure

Failure is not the opposite of success but rather a stepping stone on the path to it. It is a natural and necessary part of growth and learning, providing valuable lessons and insights that cannot be gained through success alone. By reframing failure as an opportunity for growth and learning, we can transform setbacks into springboards for future success. In my secondary school days, one of my teachers said something to the class, "Mr I can't do it ended up achieving nothing, while Mr I can try ended up achieving more than they thought was possible." The truth is that you do not try and have already failed in that venture because you never even started in the first place. Michael Faraday has failed thousands of times and recorded all these failures. He was not always so successful; he was asked to make glass. He tried for many months but was unsuccessful in the end. He was the son of a blacksmith and hated his job, but his patience paid off after time, showing that even the greatest scientific minds are not good at everything! Do you know how many times Edison failed to invent the bulb? We can go and buy a light bulb quite casually at a shop. Imagine failing 2774 times to buy one. Yes! He failed 2774 times, according to his records, and then reached a working design of an electric light bulb.[14]

Embracing Failure as a Learning Opportunity

Rather than fearing failure, embrace it as an inevitable and valuable part of the learning process. Reflect on past failures and setbacks

---

[14] Steve Nathans-Kelly, 'Live Sports Streaming and the Edison Tone Test.', *Streaming Media* 21, no. 1 (2024): 3–4.

to identify lessons learned, areas for improvement, and growth opportunities. Embrace a growth mindset that sees failure as a temporary setback rather than a permanent defeat and views challenges as opportunities for learning and development. This was particularly key for me, especially when I received grades that I was not happy with from my lecturers or supervisors. Although I was not pleased with my grades, I went the extra mile to ask for either verbal or written feedback to highlight my areas of strengths and weaknesses. This helped me develop myself in my weak areas while also noting my key areas of strength as possible pointers for where my career could be headed. I remember the first time I failed at school; I literally cried my eyes out. I was this student who always came first in class, and I could not imagine myself failing at anything. However, this was the most important lesson I learned in my life. That heralded a light bulb moment that showed me how failure could become a useful tool in the hands of someone always willing to learn and improve. When milk gets fermented, it turns to yoghurt and in some cases cheese which are both more valuable than milk.[15] When grapes ferment, they become wine which is more expensive than grape juice. What these examples show you — is that true value does not necessarily come from perfection but from the so-called imperfections and errors. Embrace your flaws and learn from them and watch yourself evolve into a valuable product on the shelf; a highly sought after commodity in the marketplace.

---

[15] Microbe Safari, 'Cheese and Yoghurt', *Microbe Safari* (blog), accessed 12 August 2024, https://microbe-safari.org.uk/food-production/cheese-and-yoghurt-production/.

Building Resilience

Resilience is the ability to bounce back from adversity, setbacks, and challenges stronger than before. Cultivate resilience by developing coping strategies, seeking support from others, and maintaining a positive outlook in the face of adversity. Practise self-care and stress management techniques to build emotional and mental resilience and cultivate a sense of purpose and meaning that provides strength and motivation during difficult times. Following on from my first-ever failure at school, while I was distraught at the time, I remember my parents saying to me that they were proud of me. It did not sound right because I felt I had somehow failed them. However, hearing those comforting words gave me the strength to forge ahead and complete my first degree with good grades. At that point, I realised the important role of having the right people around me during setbacks and challenges. The voice in your ear can be why you forge ahead or take a detour in your journey to master your career. Also, learn to build your self-esteem by constantly affirming your achievements and realising that success or failure does not define you, but your response to them and how well you persevere is what does.

Learning from Failure

Failure provides valuable insights and lessons that can inform future actions and decisions. Reflect on past failures to identify patterns, root causes, and areas for improvement. Ask yourself what you can learn from the experience, how you can grow and develop as a result, and what changes you can make to increase your chances of success in the future. Use failure as a catalyst for innovation, creativity, and growth, and embrace a mindset of continuous improvement and learning. I often tell my mentees that without ever failing, your life will be boring without an interesting story. Have you ever read a book without any anti-climax points or played a video game at the beginner level? How do you feel when something is so easy? You feel mentally unstimulated, don't you? Exactly! Humans were made to face challenges and sometimes fail, as failure is part of the plan and process of becoming. It is important to see success and failure as experiences rather than outcomes. By adopting this mindset, you set yourself up to be willing to learn from failures and make lemonades when life gives you lemons.

Resilience in Action

Resilience is demonstrated not only in how we respond to failure but also in how we persevere in the face of adversity. Draw inspiration from stories of resilience and perseverance and learn from individuals who have overcome significant challenges to achieve success. Cultivate resilience by focusing on solutions rather than problems, maintaining a sense of optimism and hope, and seeking support from others when needed. This is significantly buttressed in the Holy Scriptures by various stories of notable Bible characters who persevered amid adversity. The stories of Abraham, Jacob, Joseph, David, Job, Jesus, The Apostles, etc., give us various perspectives on the importance of resilience.[16] We should remember that wine comes from the crushing of grapes, pressure produces diamonds, and gold is refined under intense heat. The

---

[16] Bible, 'New Living Translation'.

true value of something is discovered after it has passed through rigorous processes necessary for its refinement. Similarly, our career stories are not poised to be like steady linear or exponential growth graphs. However, there are likely to be pitfalls along the way, but we can determine how the next chapter pans out with our reaction to failure and perseverance when adversity presents itself.

Summary

Failure is not the end of the road but rather a stepping stone on the path to success. By embracing failure as a learning opportunity, building resilience in the face of adversity, and learning from setbacks, we can transform challenges into opportunities for growth and development. Cultivate a mindset of resilience, perseverance, and continuous learning, and embrace failure as a natural and valuable part of the journey towards success.

Career Mastery Exercise

Understanding Failure

1. **Reflect on Past Failures:** Think about a time when you experienced failure. What did you learn from the experience?
   - Exercise: Write a brief reflection on a specific failure, detailing what happened, what you learned, and how it has impacted your growth.

2. **Reframe Failure:** Practise reframing failure as a necessary part of the journey towards success.
   - Exercise: Make a list of famous individuals who failed before succeeding and note how their failures contributed to their eventual success.

Embracing Failure as a Learning Opportunity

1. **Identify Lessons Learned:** Reflect on past failures to identify key lessons and areas for improvement.
   - Exercise: Choose a recent failure and write down at least three lessons you learned from the experience.

2. **Adopt a Growth Mindset:** Shift your perspective to view failure as an opportunity for growth and learning.
   - Exercise: Read "Mindset: The New Psychology of Success" by Carol Dweck to deepen your understanding of the growth mindset.

3. **Seek Feedback:** Ask for feedback on your failures to gain additional insights.
   - Exercise: Approach a mentor or trusted colleague and request feedback on a recent setback. Reflect on their insights and incorporate them into your improvement plan.

Building Resilience

1. **Develop Coping Strategies:** Identify and implement coping strategies to help you manage stress and bounce back from setbacks.
   - Exercise: Make a list of activities that help you relax and recharge. Schedule at least one of these activities into your weekly routine.

2. **Seek Support:** Surround yourself with supportive individuals who can provide encouragement and perspective.

- o Exercise: Identify three people in your support network who you can turn to during challenging times. Reach out to them regularly.

3. **Maintain a Positive Outlook:** Cultivate a positive mindset by focusing on solutions rather than problems.
   - o Exercise: Practise daily gratitude by writing down three things you are grateful for each day.

Learning from Failure

1. **Analyse Past Failures:** Conduct a thorough analysis of past failures to identify patterns and root causes.
   - o Exercise: Choose a significant failure and perform a SWOT analysis (Strengths, Weaknesses, Opportunities, Threats) to gain deeper insights.

2. **Set Improvement Goals:** Use the insights gained from your analysis to set specific, actionable goals for improvement.
   - o Exercise: Write down three specific goals you want to achieve based on the lessons learned from your failures.

3. **Embrace Continuous Improvement:** Commit to a mindset of continuous learning and development.
   - o Exercise: Create a personal development plan that outlines your goals, the steps you need to take to achieve them, and a timeline for completion.

Resilience in Action

1. **Draw Inspiration:** Learn from stories of resilience and perseverance to inspire your own journey.

- o Exercise: Research and write about a person who overcame significant challenges to achieve success. Reflect on what you can learn from their story.

2. **Focus on Solutions:** When faced with adversity, focus on finding solutions rather than dwelling on problems.
   - o Exercise: Identify a current challenge you are facing and brainstorm three potential solutions. Choose one and take action on it.

3. **Seek Help When Needed:** Do not be afraid to ask for help and support when facing difficulties.
   - o Exercise: Make a list of resources (people, books, online courses) that you can turn to for help and support in overcoming challenges.

WORK-LIFE BALANCE

Prioritising Self-Care and Avoiding Burnout

Introduction

Due to the current enormous demands in most workplaces, achieving a healthy work-life balance is essential for overall well-being and success. This section explores the importance of prioritising self-care and strategies for maintaining balance and avoiding burnout in personal and professional life.

> "All work and no play makes Jack a dull boy."

Understanding Work-Life Balance

Work-life balance is the equilibrium between work and personal life demands, allowing individuals to fulfil their professional responsibilities while enjoying personal pursuits, relationships, and leisure activities. Achieving balance involves setting boundaries, managing priorities, and allocating time and energy effectively to maintain overall well-being and satisfaction. Since the advent of the COVID-19 pandemic, we have witnessed an upsurge in remote working among several organisations globally. From my personal experience, I can attest to the fact that it has enhanced my work-life balance. Hours spent travelling to and from work daily can be spent to have an hour or two more of additional sleep or sorting out chores around the house. Additionally, as a dad who has just had a baby added to the family, it offers me more chances to be present for my family when needed without affecting the quality of my work. I also do not have to mention the financial benefits in terms of savings related to travel costs whenever I go to work. While I appreciate that some workplaces or occupations may not offer you the luxury of working from home, you can still take time to balance your work-leisure time. Once you get back home, that laptop should be shut, and that is it. Family time should not be compromised for other engagements, as those are precious moments that make you fulfilled and recharge you to go again in the pursuit of your career aspirations. Ensure that you create a fine distinction between work and personal life to get the most out of yourself.

The Importance of Self-Care

Self-care prioritises one's physical, emotional, and mental health needs to prevent burnout and maintain resilience. It encompasses exercise, nutrition, sleep, relaxation, and leisure pursuits that replenish energy, reduce stress, and promote overall well-being. Prioritising self-care is essential for sustaining high performance, creativity, and satisfaction in both personal and professional life.

An important factor that I incorporated into my daily life was having a routine. I discovered that when I do not have a well-planned routine for any day, I end up chasing the day, and suddenly, 24 hours is not enough. For instance, I might dedicate time for my prayers in the morning, go to the gym afterwards, shower, go through my calendar for the day, have breakfast, and then prepare for work. If I have any quick run-around, I could schedule them during my break. If I have other engagements, I schedule them after working hours. This has also helped me know when I am available for any ad hoc calls or meetings, which are not normally part of my day. Be intentional about planning your daily routine, as having a fantastic day can start with ensuring you make your bed that morning (I learnt this during my secondary school days in the Nigerian Navy). I also learnt how important physical, mental, emotional, and spiritual health are all intertwined and how a deficiency in one can spiral into others. Therefore, remember to always take care of each of these aspects. If you go to the gym but do not care for your mental health, you will soon feel exhausted and vice versa. I have also highlighted the importance of creating a reward system for yourself. This could be in the form of eating out, watching movies, relaxing, travelling for a holiday, etc. Whatever tickles your fancy, go for it, but always remember that all work and no play make Jack a dull boy!

Strategies for Maintaining Balance

- **Set Boundaries:** Establish clear boundaries between work and personal life, including designated work hours, breaks, and time for relaxation and leisure activities.

- **Prioritise Tasks:** Identify priorities and focus on high-value activities that align with your goals and values, delegating or eliminating less essential tasks.
- **Time Management:** Use time management techniques such as prioritisation, scheduling, and blocking to allocate time effectively and minimise distractions.
- **Flexibility:** Embrace flexibility and adaptability in balancing work and personal commitments, allowing for spontaneity and adjustment as needed.
- **Communication:** Communicate openly with colleagues, supervisors, and family members about your boundaries, needs, and availability to manage expectations and avoid conflicts.
- **Technology Use:** Set limits on technology use and establish boundaries for checking emails, messages, and notifications to prevent work from encroaching on personal time.

Recognising Signs of Burnout

Burnout is a state of physical, emotional, and mental exhaustion resulting from chronic stress and overwhelm. Common signs of burnout include fatigue, cynicism, decreased productivity, and feelings of detachment or apathy towards work. It is important to recognise these signs early and take proactive steps to address them before they escalate. As I write this, I am on the brink of burning out due to increasing demands from one of my life engagements. Just thinking about it, I can clearly see why it escalated to that point. When you keep pouring out into something without allowing yourself to refill, you will run out of steam, as you have little or nothing else to offer. However, you do not need to get to this point. I have noticed that in the bid to try to be always busy to avoid the guilt of life passing me by, I might get into the habit of not creating some time to refresh myself. I constantly get consumed by the thoughts of what I have not yet done and, in a short time, get overwhelmed by the fact that I have not done them. This makes me resent things I have dedicated my time to, as it may seem as if they are taking up all my time. It is okay to have things pending, and you can get back to them later. While writing this book, I had days where I was tempted to finish the entire book in a day, but I rather thought it would be better to chip away one day at a time than risk burnout and abandon the entire project.

Preventing Burnout

- **Practise Self-Awareness:** Tune into your physical, emotional, and mental state regularly, and pay attention to signs of stress and burnout.
- **Set Realistic Expectations:** Manage expectations for yourself and others, setting achievable, sustainable, and realistic goals and deadlines.
- **Seek Support:** Reach out to friends, family members, colleagues, or professional counsellors for support, encouragement, and guidance during challenging times.
- **Take Breaks:** Prioritise daily breaks to rest, recharge, and rejuvenate, allowing time for relaxation, hobbies, and leisure activities.
- **Engage in Meaningful Activities:** Pursue activities and interests outside of work that bring joy, fulfilment, and a sense of purpose, nourishing the soul and providing a source of resilience during difficult times.

Summary

Achieving work-life balance requires intentionality, self-awareness, and proactive management of priorities and boundaries. By prioritising self-care, recognising signs of burnout, and implementing strategies for maintaining balance, individuals can cultivate resilience, well-being, and satisfaction in both personal and professional life. Embrace the journey of finding balance as an ongoing process of self-discovery and growth, and prioritise your health and happiness as essential components of a fulfilling life.

Career Mastery Exercise

Understanding Work-Life Balance

1. **Assess Your Current Balance:** Evaluate how well you currently balance your work and personal life.
   - Exercise: Create a pie chart showing how you allocate your time each week between work, family, leisure, and self-care. Identify areas where you need to make adjustments.

2. **Set Work-Life Boundaries:** Establish clear boundaries between work and personal time.
   - Exercise: Write down specific boundaries you will set, such as designated work hours, break times, and personal time. Commit to sticking to these boundaries.

The Importance of Self-Care

1. **Identify Self-Care Activities:** List activities that help you relax and recharge.
   - Exercise: Create a self-care plan that includes daily, weekly, and monthly activities such as exercise, hobbies, meditation, and socialising.

2. **Establish a Routine:** Develop a daily routine that prioritises self-care.
   - Exercise: Plan a daily schedule that includes time for exercise, meals, breaks, and relaxation. Stick to this routine consistently to maintain your well-being.

Strategies for Maintaining Balance

1. **Set Boundaries:** Define clear boundaries between work and personal life.
   - Exercise: Identify specific times of the day when you will stop working and focus on personal activities. Communicate these boundaries to your colleagues and family.

2. **Prioritise Tasks:** Focus on high-value activities that align with your goals and values.
   - Exercise: Create a prioritised task list each morning. Identify the most important tasks to complete and delegate or postpone less critical ones.

3. **Time Management:** Use effective time management techniques.
   - Exercise: Implement the Pomodoro Technique by working for 25 minutes, then taking a 5-minute break.

Repeat this cycle to maintain productivity and avoid burnout.

4. **Embrace Flexibility:** Be adaptable and open to changes in your schedule.
   o Exercise: Identify areas where you can be more flexible in your routine. Adjust your plans when necessary to accommodate unexpected events.

5. **Limit Technology Use:** Set boundaries for checking emails and messages.
   o Exercise: Schedule specific times to check and respond to emails. Avoid checking work messages during personal time.

Recognising Signs of Burnout

1. **Self-Awareness:** Tune into your physical, emotional, and mental state regularly.
   o Exercise: Keep a journal to track your energy levels, mood, and stress levels daily. Look for patterns and signs of burnout.

2. **Recognise Symptoms:** Learn the common signs of burnout, such as fatigue, cynicism, and decreased productivity.
   o Exercise: Write down any symptoms you are experiencing that may indicate burnout. Reflect on what might be causing these symptoms.

Preventing Burnout

1. **Practise Self-Awareness:** Regularly check in with yourself to monitor stress levels.
   - Exercise: Set aside time each day for self-reflection. Use this time to assess your well-being and make necessary adjustments to your routine.

2. **Set Realistic Expectations:** Manage your workload by setting achievable goals.
   - Exercise: Review your current goals and deadlines. Adjust them to be more realistic and manageable if needed.

3. **Seek Support:** Reach out to friends, family, or a counsellor for help.
   - Exercise: Identify three people you can turn to for support during challenging times. Schedule regular check-ins with them.

4. **Take Regular Breaks:** Incorporate breaks into your daily schedule.
   - Exercise: Schedule short breaks throughout your workday. Use this time to step away from your desk, stretch, and relax.

5. **Engage in Meaningful Activities:** Pursue hobbies and interests outside of work.
   - Exercise: Identify activities that bring you joy and fulfilment. Make time for these activities each week to nourish your soul and reduce stress.

MANAGING IMPOSTER SYNDROME

—·—

*Recognising Your Achievements
and Building Confidence*

Introduction

Imposter syndrome is a pervasive feeling of inadequacy or self-doubt despite evidence of success or competence. This section will explore strategies for recognising your achievements, overcoming self-doubt, and building confidence to combat imposter syndrome and thrive in your personal and professional life.

> *"As a man thinketh in his heart, so is he."*
>
> **- Proverbs 23:7 KJV**

Understanding Imposter Syndrome

Imposter syndrome is characterised by feelings of self-doubt, insecurity, and fear of being exposed as a fraud despite evidence of competence and accomplishment. It often manifests as a persistent belief that one's success is due to luck or external factors rather than one's own abilities. Recognising the signs of imposter syndrome is the first step towards overcoming it and reclaiming your sense of self-worth and confidence. I will be vulnerable here; I have been severely impacted by imposter syndrome for a large part of my life. From childhood, I have always felt that anything I achieved, no matter how mind-blowing it might seem, has "solely" been a function of luck or, as we Christians will say, God's grace. I have never truly believed I was good enough to do most things. Sometimes, I stop and ask myself, "what are you the best at? You are good at many things, but what will you say is your standout gift? What is your purpose?" These questions have plagued my mind for decades, and the longer they lingered, the more I did not realise how they affected me in the long run. I get the shivers when I'm about to have a job interview, a meeting with a client, deliver a presentation, or discuss any topic. I mean, look at my resume and realise that I am not someone short of skill, experience, training, or knowledge about things to do with my career. I thrive and excel when it comes to communication, public speaking, training, people management etc. Then why do I feel that way most of the time? Some may argue that it might be due to my belief that God helps me do everything, making me doubt myself. But should it really? On the contrary, one of my favourite Bible Scriptures, Philippians 4:19, says, "I can do all things through Christ that strengthens me."[17] This should give me confidence going into anything, but you can see how the battle in our minds can wrongly interpret certain positive information and feed us negative thoughts instead. If what I have explained here is that you are not alone, keep reading to see how you can overcome this.

Recognising Your Achievements

Take time to acknowledge and celebrate your accomplishments, no matter how small or insignificant they may seem. Keep a journal or list of achievements to remind yourself of your successes and contributions. Reflect on the challenges you've overcome, the skills you've developed, and the impact you've made in your personal and professional life. For me, I just had to accept what I had achieved so far in my life. There is a song we sing that says, "Count your blessings, name them one by one." If you have read this book till this point, you can clearly see I am someone who has been through several trying moments and come through them successfully. The important thing to note here, however, is that you need to log these moments because they will serve as ardent reminders for times when imposter syndrome might want to rear its head. In my home office, I have a few certificates on the wall, along with pictures of my beautiful achievements and family. I could be working some days and feel exhausted, but when I look up and see these pictures, they remind me why I am doing what I do and why I am more than capable of achieving whatever I put my mind to.

---

[17] Bible.

Challenging Negative Self-Talk

Identify and challenge negative self-talk and limiting beliefs that contribute to feelings of imposter syndrome. Replace self-critical thoughts with positive affirmations and reminders of your strengths, capabilities, and past successes. Practise self-compassion and kindness towards yourself, recognising that everyone sometimes experiences self-doubt and insecurity. "As a man thinketh in his heart, so is he," says Proverbs 23:7 KJV.[18] The biggest enemy you can ever have in your journey to greatness is yourself. If the whole world believes in you, but you choose not to believe in yourself, your mission is dead on arrival. This is why the mind is the most vital factor in your journey to becoming because until you can conceptualise where you are going, you cannot even start the journey. I have had times when I have truly questioned my abilities, not from a place of incompetence or lack of past success, but from deeper issues concerning my self-worth. How do I know this? I might know about a certain topic or concept, but because I do not want to be embarrassed, I will either keep quiet or make suggestive statements to imply that I'm not too sure. However, when I started practising self-affirmation and declaring what I believed I was capable of to myself, I started noticing that I had this sudden pump of confidence. Sometimes, this could also be after I have listened to a motivational speech on self-doubt, listened to testimonies of others, read the Bible, prayed to God, or even listened to inspirational music. Have you noticed that sometimes, the TV shows, movies, or music you watch or listen to might have a big impact on how you perceive yourself? Yes, in fact, before these

---

[18] King James Bible, *King James Bible*, vol. 19 (Proquest LLC, 1996).

arts are created, the creators of these arts have certain ideas, positive or negative, that they are trying to communicate to their listeners or viewers. Therefore, you must be extremely careful of what you let into your mind. As the writer of Proverbs 4:23, NLT says, "Guard your heart above all else, for it determines the course of your life."[19]

Seeking External Validation

Seek feedback and validation from trusted mentors, colleagues, and friends who can provide objective perspectives and affirm your accomplishments. Share your concerns and insecurities with supportive individuals who can offer encouragement, reassurance, and constructive feedback to help you gain perspective and confidence. One factor that helped me overcome imposter syndrome was that I constantly sought the feedback of my wife, parents, mentors, or close friends whenever I had doubts about my abilities. This helped me detach myself from the picture and see myself through the lenses of others. Surprisingly, after hearing some of the words about myself, I had to challenge myself to ask why I ever thought lowly of myself. I am not saying that you always need to seek external validation to be confident in yourself. However, it could be a good starting point when you begin the journey of recovering from imposter syndrome. I like to call it "facing your fears" because, at the end of the day, imposter syndrome is embedded in fears of what others might think of you. But when you realise that you are the one just building walls in your head around your strengths and abilities, that knowledge

---

[19] Bible, 'New Living Translation'.

empowers you to break free from the shackles of self-doubt or low self-esteem.

Setting Realistic Expectations

Set realistic expectations for yourself and others, recognising perfection is unattainable and making mistakes is a natural part of the learning process. Embrace the "good enough" concept and focus on progress rather than perfection. Break tasks down into manageable steps and celebrate incremental progress towards your goals. Rome was not built in a day.[20] We often put immense pressure on ourselves by setting unrealistic expectations. More critically, these expectations might be set using the wrong metrics, e.g., what you see from social media, friends, colleagues, societal standards, etc. When you start comparing yourself to others and setting targets based on their achievements, you have just taken a detour from your own life path and started living another person's life. Nobody can do you more than you, and when you try to become another person and fail at it, you get frustrated at yourself and that person. It is important again to identify your own vision by setting SMART short and long-term goals, introspect to see the tools you currently have and lack within yourself to achieve them, identify ways to obtain the skills you still require and determine the path to get there.

---

[20] George H Sullivan, *Not Built in a Day: Exploring the Architecture of Rome* (Da Capo Press, 2006).

Building Confidence Through Action

Take action despite feelings of fear or self-doubt, recognising that confidence is built through experience and practice. Step outside your comfort zone, take on new challenges and embrace opportunities for growth and learning. Focus on the process rather than the outcome, and celebrate your courage and resilience in facing challenges head-on. A journey of a thousand miles starts with a step. The hardest part about any project is starting because that is where you have all the doubts about whether you will be successful or not. I remember when I started driving a car in Nigeria; my fear of driving left immediately after I got in the driver's seat and stepped on the throttle. However, I felt the most fear during the days leading up to that moment as I thought about the worst possible outcomes of crashing the car, getting injured or even dying. Even in my career, it was a split-moment decision where I took the bull by the horns and turned my life around when I chose to relocate to the UK for my master's degree. I had fears about studying for a postgraduate degree in oil and gas when I did not even have an undergraduate degree in that field. In fact, my colleagues on the first day of lectures were all working professionals in the oil and gas sector, and they kept interacting and engaging throughout the class session. I remember feeling overwhelmed and walking up to my lecturer for that module and asking if it was possible to get my school fees back because I thought I had made the wrong decision. However, he replied to me in these exact words, "Students like you always end up having the best results." I pondered on that statement for a long time and then realised that he meant that because I was unfamiliar with the course, I would put more effort than those who felt they knew it already. And guess what? That course was my best module, and he became my project supervisor. After that, I received the Best Project/Dissertation award from the faculty. According to Nike's slogan, just do it![21]

Cultivating a Growth Mindset

Adopt a growth mindset that sees challenges and setbacks as opportunities for learning and growth rather than indicators of failure or inadequacy. Embrace the belief that your abilities and intelligence can be developed through effort and perseverance, and view failures as valuable learning experiences that contribute to your personal and professional growth. I have said earlier in this book that you cannot expect to go to a new class year without first passing an examination. Growth comes with tests, trials, and challenges; in fact, this is what makes the growth process exciting. I will have nothing to tell you today without the ups and downs I have faced throughout my career journey to date. I have always likened the growth process to two key phenomena: plant growth and building construction. You cannot compare a palm tree's roots or height to a rose flower's. The depth of its roots determines the height of the palm tree, and the same applies to the rose flower. For the height the palm tree must grow, it needs massive roots for its nutrition, stability, and structural integrity. It may take ten to twenty years for the palm to attain its full height, ranging from seven to twelve meters,[22] while a rose flower will most likely reach its full

---

[21] NIKE, 'NIKE, Inc.', 2024, https://about.nike.com/en.

[22] Gardening Express, 'Care Guide: Growing Palm Trees in British Gardens', Gardening Express Knowledge Hub, 2023, https://help.gardeningexpress.co.uk/knowledge-base/how-to-grow-palm-trees/.

size and optimum bloom production in three to four years.[23] For similar reasons, the foundation of a skyscraper is deeper than that of a bungalow due to the height of both buildings and their structural requirements. In the same vein, we cannot compare our growth rate to others because our makeups and destinations are different. The higher you wish to go in life, the more time and resources you must invest in your developmental phases.

Summary

Managing imposter syndrome requires self-awareness, self-compassion, and a willingness to challenge negative self-talk and limiting beliefs. By recognising your achievements, seeking external validation, setting realistic expectations, building confidence through action, and cultivating a growth mindset, you can overcome imposter syndrome and realise your full potential. Embrace your worthiness and capabilities, and trust your ability to succeed in your personal and professional endeavours.

Career Mastery Exercise

Understanding Imposter Syndrome

1. **Identify Imposter Thoughts:** Reflect on moments when you've felt like an imposter. What triggered these feelings?
   - Exercise: Write down a recent experience where you felt self-doubt or inadequacy. Identify the thoughts and emotions associated with it.

---

[23] Epic Gardening, 'Rose Growth Stages: How Fast Do Roses Grow?', 2023, https://www.epicgardening.com/rose-growth-stages/.

2. **Acknowledge Your Feelings:** Understand that imposter syndrome is common and affects many successful people.
   - o Exercise: Read articles or watch videos of successful individuals who have experienced imposter syndrome. Reflect on their stories and draw parallels to your own experiences.

Recognising Your Achievements

1. **Celebrate Your Successes:** Keep a journal or list of your accomplishments, big and small.
   - o Exercise: Write down three achievements you are proud of. Reflect on the skills, effort, and dedication it took to achieve them.

2. **Visual Reminders:** Create visual reminders of your accomplishments to boost your confidence.
   - o Exercise: Display your certificates, awards, or any visual representation of your achievements in your workspace.

Challenging Negative Self-Talk

1. **Identify Negative Self-Talk:** Pay attention to your inner dialogue and identify self-critical thoughts.
   - o Exercise: Keep a journal for a week and note instances of negative self-talk. Challenge these thoughts by writing down evidence that contradicts them.

2. **Positive Affirmations:** Replace negative thoughts with positive affirmations.
   - o Exercise: Write down five positive affirmations about your abilities and strengths. Repeat them daily, especially during moments of self-doubt.

Seeking External Validation

1. **Ask for Feedback:** Seek feedback from trusted colleagues, mentors, or friends to gain objective perspectives.
   - Exercise: Request feedback on a recent project or task. Reflect on the positive aspects mentioned and areas for improvement.

2. **Share Your Concerns:** Open up to someone you trust about your feelings of self-doubt.
   - Exercise: Schedule a conversation with a mentor or trusted friend to discuss your imposter syndrome. Note their reassurances and advice.

Setting Realistic Expectations

1. **Set Achievable Goals:** Break down your tasks into manageable steps and set realistic deadlines.
   - Exercise: Choose a goal and break it into smaller, actionable steps. Create a timeline for achieving each step.

2. **Embrace Imperfection:** Accept that perfection is unattainable and that making mistakes is part of the learning process.
   - Exercise: Reflect on a recent mistake. Write down what you learned from it and how it contributed to your growth.

Building Confidence Through Action

1. **Take Small Steps:** Confront your fears and take small steps outside your comfort zone.
   - Exercise: Identify an area where you feel self-doubt. Set a small, achievable task in that area and take action on it.

2. **Celebrate Progress:** Acknowledge and celebrate your progress, no matter how small.
   - Exercise: At the end of each week, reflect on what you have achieved and reward yourself for your efforts.

Cultivating a Growth Mindset

1. **Embrace Challenges:** View challenges as opportunities for growth and learning.
   - Exercise: Identify a current challenge you are facing. Write down what you can learn from this experience and how it can help you grow.

2. **Learn from Failure:** See failures as valuable learning experiences.
   - Exercise: Reflect on a past failure. Write down the lessons learned and how it has contributed to your personal or professional growth.

CHAPTER

FIVE

LEADERSHIP AND INFLUENCE

LEADING BY EXAMPLE

— • —

*Developing Leadership Skills Through
Collaboration and Empowerment*

Introduction

Leadership is not defined solely by titles or positions but by actions and influence. In this section, we will explore the concept of leading by example, developing leadership skills through collaboration and empowerment, and fostering a culture of growth and excellence within teams and organisations.

"Never let success get to your head, or failure get to your heart."

- Anthony Joshua

Understanding Leading by Example

Leading by example is a leadership approach emphasising modelling behaviours, values, and attitudes that inspire and motivate others to follow suit. It involves demonstrating integrity, authenticity, and accountability in actions and decisions and serving as a role model for ethical conduct, professionalism, and excellence. We all know of the saying, "Practise what you preach." It is easier said than done when you do not put yourself in the shoes of those you manage or lead. The issue arises when, as a leader, you have little to no idea of the technicalities of your team's work. This creates a disjoint between the team and yourself, and sometimes, some mischievous team members might use that against you by sabotaging a project, knowing that you have no idea how to fix it. I encourage my mentees to be knowledgeable in any jobs they apply for and try to upskill themselves in areas they might feel deficient in. When you are competent, you carry out your work with confidence, and you can defend the quality of your outputs, which also reflects on the performance of the team you lead. I must point out here that we also must be able to switch between various leadership modes when we show up to our teams.[24] Sometimes, we might have to be in *"operator mode,"* where we get involved in executing actions, being task-oriented and focused on short-term goals. There are other times when we might plug into our *"manager mode,"* where our attention is channelled more towards directing, delegating, prioritising, planning, analysing, supervising, and controlling the flow of the work at hand and team performance. It could also be that we are sometimes in *"leader*

---

[24] Anthony Landale, 'Anyone Can Make a Bigger Difference', *Manager*, 2010, 28.

mode," which involves more of looking at the long-term vision of a project, defining purpose, culture, relationships, context, responsibility, and inspiration to ensure you have an oversight that things are going on the right track. Depending on the circumstances, we could show up to work in different modes, so do not make the false assumption that any mode is more important than the other. Be sensitive to identify what your team needs at every point.

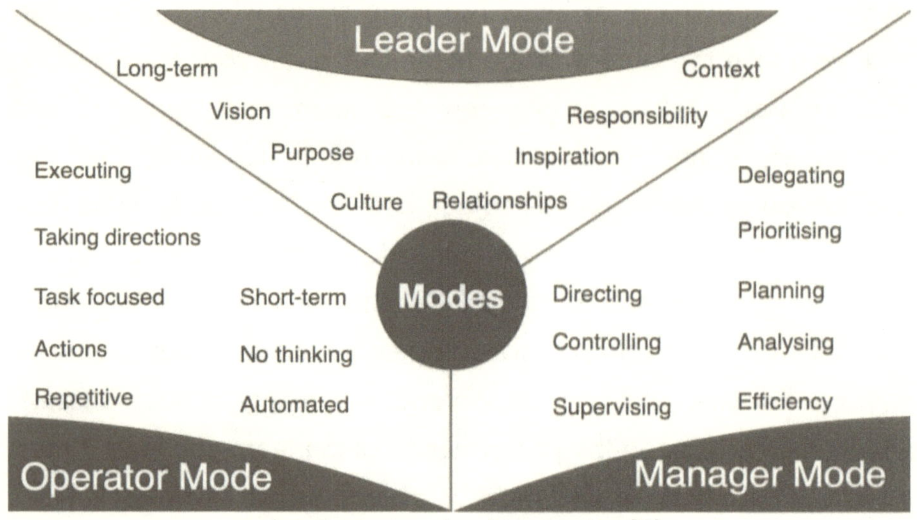

The Three Leadership Modes [28]

The Power of Collaboration

Collaboration is a cornerstone of effective leadership, enabling individuals to leverage diverse perspectives, skills, and experiences to achieve common goals. Encourage open communication, active listening, and mutual respect within teams, fostering an environment where everyone feels valued and empowered to contribute their ideas and insights. Again, pardon me for always referring to Biblical Scriptures, as I am most familiar with this as a Christian. Some Bible verses come to mind when I think about the power of collaboration.[25] "Can two people walk together without agreeing on the direction?" Amos 3:3 NLT. When we also examine Deuteronomy 32:30, Joshua 23:10, and Isaiah 30:17, we can see the exponential effect of one person chasing a thousand and two chasing ten thousand. This tells us how vital collaboration is to any vision or goal. In fact, most of the time, when I am in doubt, I know have a supportive team, and I feel confident and empowered to make informed and calculated decisions, as I know I trust the team around me to offer valuable support.

Empowering Others

Empowerment is the process of delegating authority, responsibility, and decision-making power to individuals, enabling them to take ownership of their work and contribute to organisational success. Empowerment builds trust, confidence, and accountability within teams, fostering a culture of autonomy, innovation, and continuous improvement. As a leader, assigning tasks to team members according to their competencies is also important. One tool that has been instrumental in helping me delegate effectively is the Belbin team roles questionnaire, which groups individuals within teams into: - Resource Investigator, Team worker, Co-ordinator, Plant, Monitor Evaluator, Specialist, Shaper, Implementer and Completer Finisher.[26] When my teams complete the Belbin questionnaires, it helps me understand their strengths

---

[25] Bible, 'New Living Translation'.
[26] Meredith Belbin, 'The Nine Belbin Team Roles', 1981, https://www.belbin.com/about/belbin-team-roles.

and weaknesses and where they will fit in and excel in a particular project. I always recommend courses to team members to help them develop their career paths. Try to understand the career aspirations of your team members, as this will help you create a developmental plan for them and guide them in their career journey, making them feel more valued within the team. As a leader, I must point out that you should never feel threatened by the successes of your mentees or team members, and if you have observed that this does happen, then you must introspect to identify if there are any internal battles with low self-esteem or confidence in your abilities. Instead, see your team members as a project which you have taken on to make better. The better they are, the better you are.

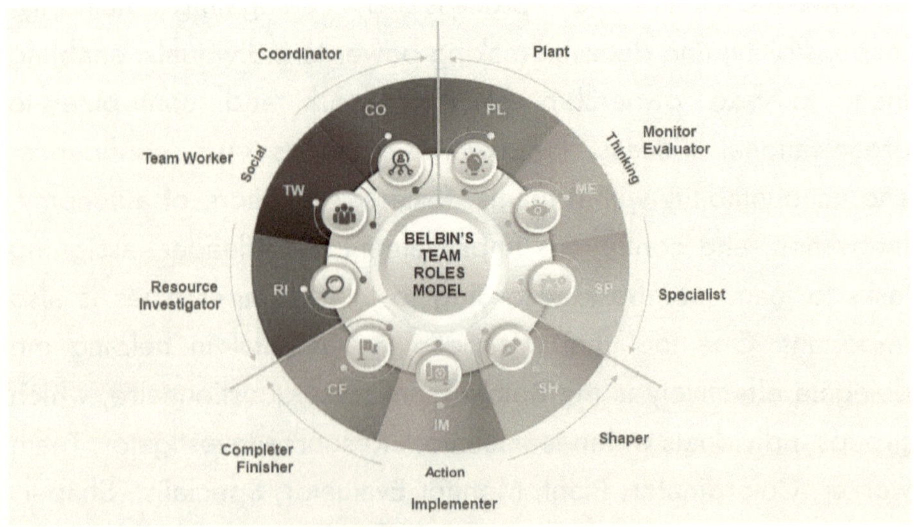

The Nine Belbin team roles [25]

Developing Leadership Skills

Developing leadership skills requires self-awareness, self-reflection, and a commitment to lifelong learning and growth. Identify areas for development, set goals, and seek opportunities to enhance your leadership capabilities through training, mentorship, and hands-on experience. Practise empathy, emotional intelligence, and effective communication to build strong relationships and inspire trust and confidence in others. The 360-degree leadership assessment feedback tool has proven useful in gathering feedback from my colleagues and team members about my strengths and weaknesses, which then help me identify potential areas of improvement based on scoring metrics and comments from my team.[27] I have also used feedback from this tool to enrol in courses that will enhance my abilities in areas where I lack certain competencies, while also gaining an understanding of what my team thinks of me. I reckon this is important because our perception of ourselves can often times be subjective, but giving people an opportunity to offer you anonymous feedback means that you get the true reflection of yourself from people's perspectives without fear of them being implicated by their opinions. However, you should also be ready to receive blunt, unbiased, and harsh feedback that could give you a reality check. Nonetheless, be careful to distinguish between constructive and destructive criticism and focus on the former.

---

[27] CD McCauley et al., 'Should 360-Degree Feedback Be Used Only for Developmental Purposes', *Ix-Xii. Greensboro, NC: Center for Creative Leadership*, 1997.

Leading Through Adversity

True leadership is tested during times of adversity and uncertainty. Demonstrate resilience, adaptability, and courage in navigating challenges and setbacks, and maintain a positive attitude and outlook in adversity. Lead with empathy and compassion, supporting and uplifting others during difficult times and rallying teams around a shared vision and purpose. There were times when I was involved in projects where things were not going according to plan. However, instead of casting aspersions or blame, I took the ship's helm and steered us back in the right direction. In most job interviews, especially those with leadership roles, you will most likely get asked a question about your reaction in the face of adversity or conflict or when a task or project does not go according to plan. This question helps to give the employer some insight into your values regarding people management, conflict resolution, working under pressure, and levels of determination. Thus, as highlighted in previous chapters of this book, you can see why it is important to view failure as a learning curve rather than a result or outcome.

Celebrating Success and Learning from Failure

Celebrate successes and milestones, acknowledging the contributions of individuals and teams towards achieving shared goals. Recognise and reward achievements, fostering a culture of appreciation, recognition, and gratitude within organisations. Embrace failure as a learning opportunity, encouraging experimentation, innovation, and risk-taking, and promoting a growth mindset that values continuous learning and improvement. I want to reiterate the importance of celebrating wins and learning from losses. As someone leading a team, let us remember that focusing too much on things that are not going well might drain the energy levels within your team. I could organise an eat-out for my teams when we hit a milestone or achieve a performance target to encourage the team to do better. But guess what? Sometimes, when we do not achieve our goal, I still do the same thing, albeit this time to discuss where things went wrong and how to improve. This teaches my team members not to be overly result-oriented but also process-focused. That means they are not overly deflated when we do not perform to high standards, but at the same time, they know that there is a no-blame culture that creates transparency and willingness to learn. According to a quote from one of my role models, former two-time boxing heavyweight champion — and I dare say soon-to-be three-time champion — Anthony Joshua, "Never let success get to your head, or failure get to your heart."[28] This means you must always maintain a level head, regardless of success or failure. From a health and safety perspective, I also want to state here that as leaders, we should be careful to draw the line between incentivising our team members using lagging indicators, such as the team with the least number of safety incidents, as this might foster a culture of non-reporting when things go wrong. However, leading indicators such as teams with the best health and safety practices might encourage cross-team benchmarking and organisational learning.

---

[28] Anthony Joshua [@anthonyjoshua], "'One More Hour, One More Day, 25/8. Never Let Success Get to Your Head, or Failure to Your Heart." These Are Words I Live by and Inspiration for My New #BOSSxAJBXNG Collection. Take a Look at the New Pieces I Co-Created with the @HUGOBOSS Team #BOSSsports Https://On.Boss.Com/BOSSxAJBXNG_AJ_ Https://T.Co/BK0xtMC8MU', Tweet, *Twitter*, 2 September 2020, https://x.com/anthonyjoshua/status/1301144318347014144.

Fostering a Culture of Growth and Excellence

As a leader, cultivate a culture of growth and excellence within teams and organisations, empowering individuals to unleash their full potential and pursue excellence in everything they do. Foster a climate of trust, transparency, and accountability, where feedback is valued and used to drive continuous improvement and innovation. Lead by example, demonstrating a commitment to integrity, authenticity, and ethical conduct in all aspects of your leadership role. Let us talk a bit about leadership energies. There are four types of leadership energies: physical, intellectual, emotional, and spiritual.[29] When you discover your leadership energy, you understand the kind of leader you are and areas where you need to improve yourself because, at some point in a project phase, you may need to reflect each of these leadership energies to your team. My team has sometimes shown signs of physical demotivation or fatigue, and I have had to inject some physical energy into the room to get things done. In areas where they had seemed unsure about how to carry out a project, I have had to initiate my intellectual energy to foster innovation, analysis, and knowledge sharing. It could also be that my team might want to feel valued for the work they do to energise them to apply themselves better, for which I could organise informal team get-togethers or one-to-one sessions to build personal relationships, connection, passion, empathy, and care. Sometimes, it has also been a case of not fully understanding why we had to do a project or undertake it a certain way. This is where spiritual energy comes in to remind everyone of our values, vision, mission, and overall purpose as a

---

[29] Steve Radcliffe, *Leadership: Plain and Simple* (Pearson UK, 2012).

team. By knowing and developing your leadership energies and applying them appropriately, you could foster a culture of growth and excellence within your team. I am a huge supporter of Arsenal Football Club, and I remember when our first team manager, Mikel Arteta, joined the club. In most of his press conferences and after watching the Amazon Prime 'All or Nothing' documentary, he kept talking about transmitting energies from him to the players to the fans and vice versa. In one of his press conferences, he said, "I'm an energy giver. I don't like energy suckers - I just like to give it. I like people who give energy in many different ways. That can be through body language, tone of voice, looking for solutions and not excuses. [I bring] energy - a lot of energy."[30] I did not fully understand at the time what he meant, but in hindsight, I must say he is a genius; having implemented these four modes of leadership energies seamlessly into the Arsenal team, and the positive impact it has had for the entire club is evident for all to see.

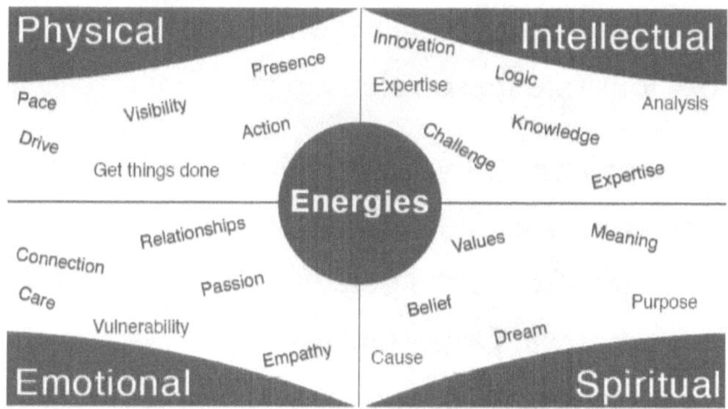

The Four Leadership energies [28]

---

30 Arsenal FC, 'Arteta on the Importance of Providing Energy', Arteta on the importance of providing energy, 10 February 2023, https://www.arsenal.com/news/arteta-importance-providing-energy.

Summary

Leading by example is a powerful leadership approach that inspires and empowers others to reach their full potential and achieve collective success. Leaders can cultivate high-performing teams and organisations that thrive in today's dynamic and competitive landscape by fostering collaboration, empowerment, and a culture of growth and excellence. Embrace the opportunity to lead by example and inspire others to become the leaders of tomorrow.

Career Mastery Exercise

Understanding Leading by Example

1. **Model the Way:** Reflect on how your actions align with your words.
   - Exercise: Identify three core values you want to embody as a leader. Write down specific behaviours that demonstrate these values in your daily actions.

2. **Self-Assessment:** Evaluate your leadership style and areas for improvement.
   - Exercise: Conduct a personal SWOT analysis (Strengths, Weaknesses, Opportunities, Threats) to gain insight into your leadership capabilities and areas for growth.

The Power of Collaboration

1. **Encourage Open Communication:** Foster an environment of transparency and respect within your team.

- o Exercise: Schedule regular team meetings where everyone has the opportunity to share their ideas and feedback. Make sure to actively listen and acknowledge contributions.

2. **Leverage Diversity:** Recognise the value of diverse perspectives and skills.
   - o Exercise: Create a project plan that assigns roles based on team members' strengths and expertise. Highlight how each member's unique skills contribute to the team's goals.

Empowering Others

1. **Delegate Authority:** Empower your team by delegating responsibilities and decision-making power.
   - o Exercise: Identify a task or project to delegate to team members using the Belbin roles questionnaire. Provide clear guidelines and support, and trust them to take ownership of the task.

2. **Develop Potential:** Invest in your team's growth and development.
   - o Exercise: Conduct one-on-one meetings with your team members to discuss their career aspirations and create individual development plans with specific goals and actions.

Developing Leadership Skills

1. **Seek Feedback:** Use tools like the 360-degree leadership assessment to gain insights into your leadership style.

- o Exercise: Request anonymous feedback from colleagues and team members. Reflect on the feedback and identify key areas for improvement.

2. **Continuous Learning:** Commit to ongoing learning and development.
   - o Exercise: Enrol in a leadership training course or read a book on leadership development. Apply the learnings to your leadership practice.

Leading Through Adversity

1. **Demonstrate Resilience:** Show strength and composure during challenging times.
   - o Exercise: Reflect on a recent adversity or setback. Write down how you handled it and what you learned. Identify strategies for demonstrating resilience in future challenges.

2. **Lead with Empathy:** Support your team through difficult times with understanding and compassion.
   - o Exercise: Practise active listening with your team members, especially during stressful periods. Offer support and resources to help them navigate challenges.

Celebrating Success and Learning from Failure

1. **Acknowledge Achievements:** Celebrate successes and recognise contributions.
   - o Exercise: Plan a team celebration or recognition event to acknowledge recent achievements. Use this time to highlight individual contributions and team effort.

2. **Promote a Growth Mindset:** Encourage learning from failures and continuous improvement.
   - o Exercise: Hold a retrospective meeting after completing a project to discuss what went well and what could be improved. Emphasise the importance of learning from mistakes.

Fostering a Culture of Growth and Excellence

1. **Cultivate Leadership Energies:** Develop and apply physical, intellectual, emotional, and spiritual leadership energies.
   - o Exercise: Identify which leadership energy you need to develop further. Create a plan to enhance this energy, such as physical activities for physical energy or team-building exercises for emotional energy.

2. **Create a Vision of Excellence:** Inspire your team with a clear and compelling vision.
   - o Exercise: Communicate your vision and goals to your team regularly. Use stories, examples, and real-life successes to illustrate the vision and motivate your team.

BUILDING YOUR BRAND

*Establishing Your Professional
Identity and Online Presence*

Introduction

In today's interconnected world, building a strong personal brand is essential for standing out in your field, attracting opportunities, and advancing your career. This section explores the importance of establishing your professional identity and creating a compelling online presence to enhance visibility, credibility, and influence.

> *"Picture yourself as a product on the shelf and internalise how you want to be visualised. This will help you create a mental picture of what your branding or packaging should look like."*

Defining Your Professional Identity

Your professional identity encompasses your skills, experiences, values, and unique personality traits that differentiate you from others in your field. Take time to reflect on your strengths, passions, and career goals to define your professional identity and articulate what sets you apart from others. I was stuck in a bubble for a long time trying to define my professional identity since I had been involved in multiple roles across diverse industry sectors, including biomedical, oil and gas, academia, healthcare, government, etc. This created a conundrum in my career development as to how I saw my next 5 years panning out due to my flexibility across multiple disciplines. However, I was keen on establishing a relationship between all my past experiences and how they had made me the astute professional I had become today. On closer examination, I observed that there were loads of transferrable skills which I had obtained from each of my previous roles that were pertinent to my career progression and development, both as a professional and business owner. This helped me reshape and redefine myself by building a story around my multifaceted life that now appeals to a diverse range of professionals globally. So, look out for the key skills that you have picked out during your education and career, and try to draw a route map of your career to date and where you are headed by identifying some transferable skills that have helped build you up in your career.

Crafting Your Personal Brand

Your personal brand is the perception that others have of you based on your actions, behaviour, and communication. Define your personal brand by identifying your core values, strengths, and areas of expertise and communicate them consistently across all channels and interactions. Develop a unique value proposition highlighting what you bring to the table and how you can solve problems or add value for others. First impressions do matter, as the saying goes. I always tell my mentees that whenever someone sees your online profile, what is the first thing they want them to think about you? This must be communicated within the first five seconds of someone going through your complimentary card, social media page, website, etc. I do not compromise on excellence and am big on content and packaging. I am not sure anyone will buy a product that has not been well packaged, regardless of how good the content is on the inside. In fact, customers will hardly pick an item on a shelf with a damaged or unpresentable package. The same thing applies to you as a career professional or businessperson. You are the face of your career or business, and you must be able to sell that image to whoever you want to patronise your product or service. You want to leave a lasting impression on an employer after an interview or a client after a meeting that makes your thoughts stick to their mind after meeting you. However, this can only be developed when you refine the package that comes with the product. This can be by enhancing your communication and interpersonal skills, dress sense (oh yes, dress how you want to be addressed), mannerisms, expanding your knowledge base by keeping abreast with global current affairs, etc. I cannot tell you how many times I have attended an interview or spoken to a client, and we ended up shaking hands on a deal or contract and hardly discussed any technicalities, but we spent our time discussing politics, sports, religion, etc. The illiterate of the 21st century is not someone who has never been in the four walls of a classroom, but someone who refuses to expand their knowledge base with up-to-date information.

Creating a Compelling Online Presence

In today's digital dispensation, your online presence plays a crucial role in shaping perceptions of your personal brand. Establish a professional online presence by creating a polished and up-to-date LinkedIn profile that showcases your skills, experiences, and achievements. Consider creating a personal website or blog to share your expertise, insights, and accomplishments and engage with others in your industry through social media platforms and online communities. The first thing you see on my LinkedIn profile is that I am a Chartered Human Factors Specialist, Registered Health and Safety Consultant, and Oil and Gas Process Safety Expert with expertise across a wide range of industry sectors. My university connections and PhD degree are also well displayed, which gives my profile visitors a quick glance at my career to date. Also, I ensure that I make or contribute to posts related to trending topics in my field, which will stir up discussion among like-minded professionals, which is another avenue for selling yourself to your industry. Be sure to also showcase excellence in the quality of pictures of yourself you upload online, especially your profile pictures. The saying "A picture says a thousand words" has never been truer when presenting yourself to an online audience. Picture yourself as a product on the shelf and internalise how you want to be visualised. This will help you create a mental picture of what your branding or packaging should look like. Also, never forget that your personal values must be reflected in your brand as most clients or employers like to buy into your person and not just your skills to ensure that you are a right fit for their team or business.

Building a Professional Network

Networking is essential for building relationships, expanding your professional network, and creating opportunities for growth and advancement. Actively engage in online and offline networking activities, such as attending industry events, joining professional organisations, and participating in online forums and discussions. Build meaningful connections with others in your field by offering value, providing support, and seeking opportunities for collaboration and mentorship. If you have noticed a common denominator in all this book has been communicating till this point, you cannot, and I repeat, be successful in your career without a good support network. Some people feel they can do it on their own, but think about it: Can you really do it? Every wealthy person on earth today acquires wealth from other people's money. They did not assume they did not need a network of clients, distributors, marketers, consumers, or even employees. People tend to downplay the importance of networks in career development because the school system has instilled it in us to be "independent." You write assignments, tests, and examinations independently, graduate with your own grades, etc. This has subconsciously instilled some level of competition among professionals and hindered meaningful collaboration where necessary. This is why one of the most meaningful assignments or projects you will most likely be involved in during your academic or professional journey will be those that require group or teamwork. These tasks will help you understand the nature of how people work, how to manage strengths and weaknesses within a team, and how to foster meaningful relationships. For the sake of emphasis, always remember that your network is your net worth.

Sharing Your Expertise Through Content Creation

Establish yourself as a thought leader by creating and sharing valuable content demonstrating your expertise and insights. Write articles, blog posts, or whitepapers on topics relevant to your industry, and share them through your website, social media channels, and professional networks. Participate in speaking engagements, webinars, or podcasts to share your knowledge and engage with audiences on a larger scale. This book is one of my proudest achievements, as it has allowed me to share most of my life experiences in a nutshell. Not only does it serve as a medium to market my wealth of skills and experience, but it is also a key reflection point for me. While writing this book, there were moments I paused and was filled with gratitude, my eyes welling up with tears, because all the years I doubted myself, I never realised I had achieved this much with a lot more to come, of course. This book has initiated a turning point in my life, and it is about how I should see myself from the outside looking in. It has also given me the drive to always journal my experiences as this could just be the help someone out there needs. Moreover, I had always had questions on my mind about what my content creation on YouTube and social media should be based on. As you can see, this book has given me the answers I have long sought.

Managing Your Online Reputation

Your online reputation reflects your personal brand and can influence how others perceive you professionally. Monitor your online presence regularly to accurately reflect your values, expertise, and achievements. Respond promptly and professionally to comments, messages, and inquiries, and address any negative feedback or criticism gracefully and professionally. Sometimes, I have applied for jobs or chatted with a client, and within minutes of doing so, I get a notification that they have sent a friend request to one of my social media accounts. The greatest delusion you will ever wrap yourself into is to think that clients or employers are not interested in your personal life. Breaking news!!! Of course they are! Your true personality is reflected in your daily life and not just how you attend work or business. Have you ever wondered why a big brand might pull out their endorsement from a celebrity when they have a scandal in their personal life? This is because one of the key elements of how multinationals operate is their Corporate Social Responsibility (especially from an ethical or human rights responsibility standpoint), which means their reputation and what they stand for represent an important metric for consumer behaviour towards their products or services. Again, ponder this question regarding your online reputation; "What would you like your brand or name to be associated with"? According to Proverbs 22:1 NKJV, "A good name is rather to be chosen than great riches, and loving favour rather than silver and gold."

Summary

Building your brand is an ongoing process of self-discovery, self-promotion, and relationship-building that requires authenticity, consistency, and dedication. By defining your professional identity, creating a compelling online presence, building a professional network, sharing your expertise through content creation, and managing your online reputation, you can establish a strong personal brand that opens doors to new opportunities and propels your career forward. Embrace the power of personal branding and leverage it as a tool for professional growth and success.

Career Mastery Exercise

Defining Your Professional Identity

1. **Reflect on Your Strengths and Values:** Consider what makes you unique and what you bring to the table.
   - Exercise: Write down your top three strengths, core values, and career goals. Reflect on how these elements shape your professional identity.

2. **Identify Transferable Skills:** Think about skills gained from past experiences that can be applied to your current or desired role.
   - Exercise: Create a list of transferable skills from your education and career. Highlight how these skills have contributed to your growth and how they can be leveraged in your future career.

Crafting Your Personal Brand

1. **Develop a Unique Value Proposition:** Clearly articulate what sets you apart and how you add value.
   - Exercise: Write a personal branding statement that summarises your unique skills, experiences, and the value you provide. Keep it concise and impactful.

2. **First Impressions Matter:** Ensure your appearance and behaviour consistently reflect your personal brand.
   - Exercise: Review your online profiles, business cards, and professional wardrobe. Ensure they align with the image you want to project.

Creating a Compelling Online Presence

1. **Enhance Your LinkedIn Profile:** Make sure your LinkedIn profile is up-to-date and highlights your achievements.
   - Exercise: Update your LinkedIn headline, summary, and work experience sections. Add a professional profile picture and banner image.

2. **Build a Personal Website:** Create a website to showcase your portfolio, blog, or professional achievements.
   - Exercise: Set up a simple personal website using platforms like WordPress or Wix. Include sections such as About Me, Portfolio, Blog, and Contact Information.

Building a Professional Network

1. **Engage in Networking Activities:** Attend industry events, join professional organisations, and participate in online forums.

o Exercise: Identify three industry events or online communities to join. Set a goal to connect with at least five new professionals each month.

2. **Offer Value to Your Network:** Build meaningful connections by offering support and seeking collaboration opportunities.

o Exercise: Reach out to someone in your network and offer assistance or propose a collaborative project. Follow up regularly to maintain the connection.

Sharing Your Expertise Through Content Creation

1. **Create and Share Valuable Content:** Establish yourself as a thought leader by sharing your knowledge and insights.

o Exercise: Write an article or blog post on a topic relevant to your industry. Share it on your website and social media platforms.

2. **Engage in Speaking Opportunities:** Participate in webinars, podcasts, or industry conferences to share your expertise.

o Exercise: Identify at least two speaking opportunities or podcasts to participate in. Prepare a presentation or talking points to showcase your knowledge.

Managing Your Online Reputation

1. **Monitor Your Online Presence:** Regularly check your online profiles and search results to ensure they accurately reflect your brand.

- o Exercise: Set up Google Alerts for your name and review your social media profiles. Update any outdated information and address any negative feedback.

2. **Respond Professionally to Feedback:** Handle comments, messages, and criticism with grace and professionalism.
   - o Exercise: Practise writing professional responses to potential negative feedback or criticism. Maintain a positive and constructive tone.

MENTORING OTHERS

—•—

*Paying It Forward and Contributing
to the Growth of Your Field*

Introduction

Mentoring is a powerful relationship that fosters growth, learning, and development for both mentees and mentors. In this section, we will explore the importance of mentoring, its benefits to individuals and the broader community, and strategies for becoming an effective mentor.

> *"You are the light of the world—like a city on a hilltop that cannot be hidden. No one lights a lamp and then puts it under a basket. Instead, a lamp is placed on a stand, giving light to everyone in the house. In the same way, let your good deeds shine out for all to see so that everyone will praise your heavenly Father."*
>
> **- Matthew 5:14-16 NLT**

Understanding the Importance of Mentoring

Mentoring is a reciprocal relationship where individuals with more experience and expertise support and guide less experienced people. Mentoring provides valuable opportunities for knowledge transfer, skill development, and professional growth, benefiting both mentees and mentors. By sharing insights, experiences, and advice, mentors contribute to the success and advancement of their mentees while also gaining fulfilment and satisfaction from supporting others. I must mention that I initially did not actively seek opportunities to become a mentor. It was more of a situation where the evidence of my works and achievements spoke for themselves, and I was approached afterwards by prospective mentees seeking mentorship. However, recently, I have started putting myself out there to mentor various professionals within my discipline and those looking to improve themselves in any areas where I have experience. One thing I have discovered from being a mentor to hundreds of aspiring and current professionals within and outside my field is that it offers me the opportunity to create an impact for the individual and the industry as a whole. I should also highlight that being in academia for a decade also allowed me to be in constant communication with students who saw themselves in my life trajectory and thought to buy into my experience through mentorship. Another value proposition of mentorship is the ability to learn and develop yourself while also developing others. I had the opportunity to reflect on my own practices sometimes when offering advice to a mentee, especially because these mentees could sometimes have questions that you, as a mentor, had never thought about. So, also learn to keep an open mind to learn when interacting with your mentees because they also have something valuable to offer you.

Benefits of Mentoring for Mentees

For mentees, mentoring provides access to guidance, support, and expertise that accelerates learning and development. Mentees benefit from personalised feedback, advice, and encouragement from experienced professionals, helping them navigate challenges, overcome obstacles, and reach their goals more effectively. Mentoring also provides mentees with valuable networking opportunities, exposure to different perspectives, and increased confidence and self-awareness. Again, reading this book up to this point, you should have realised the important role a mentor plays in a mentee's life. I have highlighted some personal examples of how mentors helped me in my education, career, personal life, etc. However, closer examination through the lens of my mentees has also pointed out vital aspects of why mentoring is important for mentees. My mentees reach out to me multiple times weekly to say how grateful they are and how my mentorship has helped them graduate with excellent grades, land their dream job, or become better people. From their feedback, they can now track their progress and see how far they have come in their career pursuits while also setting SMART goals for the years ahead. You can tell the dramatic transformation from when they had no mentorship to when they had one. Suddenly, an aspiring professional who had many doubts about navigating their education or career seems to have a confidence boost to take on any challenges and dream big with daring goals. The difference is this: the same way the words of my mentors turned my life around for the better, those same seeds have been replanted in others and have had the same effect.

Benefits of Mentoring for Mentors

For mentors, mentoring offers opportunities for personal and professional growth, as well as the satisfaction of making a positive impact on others. Mentors develop leadership and coaching skills, enhance their ability to communicate and connect with others, and gain fresh insights and perspectives from mentees. Mentoring also provides mentors with a sense of fulfilment and purpose as they contribute to the growth and success of the next generation of professionals in their field. The fulfilment I get from seeing my mentees thrive in their chosen career endeavours is compared to none. When I scroll through LinkedIn and see my mentees doing big things in their places of work or education, I get a sense of satisfaction that not only did I not waste my time with these individuals, but I have sown a seed that will surely go on to yield more fruits and benefit others who will probably never meet me in their lives. It gives me the confidence of knowing that I took on someone as a project, and it has ended up as a successful one, which also offers me a template for what works to be applied in future contexts. My future aspirations regarding nation-building, effective governance and transformational leadership are hinged and predicated on the experience I get from successfully mentoring these amazing professionals. Again, it is a win-win situation for everyone, so please do not see it as wasting your time.

Strategies for Effective Mentoring

- **Establish Clear Goals:** Define clear objectives and expectations for the mentoring relationship, outlining what both parties hope to achieve.
- **Foster Trust and Rapport:** Build a trusting and supportive relationship with your mentee, creating a safe space for open communication and feedback.
- **Provide Guidance and Support:** Offer guidance, advice, and support to your mentee based on your own experiences and expertise, helping them navigate challenges and opportunities.
- **Encourage Self-Reflection and Growth:** Encourage your mentee to reflect on their experiences, identify growth areas, and set development goals.
- **Empower and Encourage:** Empower your mentee to take ownership of their growth and development and encourage them to step outside their comfort zone and pursue new opportunities.
- **Lead by Example:** Demonstrate the behaviours, attitudes, and values you want to instil in your mentee, leading by example and serving as a positive role model.

Paying It Forward and Contributing to the Growth of Your Field

Mentoring is not just about helping individual mentees succeed; it's also about contributing to the growth and advancement of your field. By mentoring others, you help build a stronger, more resilient community of professionals equipped with the knowledge, skills, and support they need to thrive. Mentoring creates a ripple effect that extends far beyond the individual mentee, impacting organisations, industries, and society in its entirety. I have spoken about my ambitions to impact my industry nationally and globally, but these cannot happen when I cannot implement these locally. I have learnt to put myself and my knowledge out there by leveraging various media such as books, publications, social media, conferences, workshops, meetings, etc. In all fairness, the greatness you seek in life is located on the other side of mentorship. Until people can look up to you as someone who has walked a certain path and ask you for directions, you might most likely not be impacting that field. If you do not have potential mentees coming your way, start putting yourself out there by posting about your knowledge, creating that YouTube channel, writing that book, publishing that paper, starting that blog, attending that conference, and just doing whatever you know will shine the torch on the valuable unique experience you have to offer the world. You never know how valuable the content in your head is until it is put up in the marketplace.

> *"You are the light of the world—like a city on a hilltop that cannot be hidden. No one lights a lamp and then puts it under a basket. Instead, a lamp is placed on a stand, giving light to everyone in the house. In the same way, let your good deeds shine out for all to see so that everyone will praise your heavenly Father."*
>
> **Matthew 5:14-16 NLT**[31]

---

[31] Bible, 'New Living Translation'.

Summary

Mentoring is a powerful relationship that benefits both mentees and mentors, fostering growth, learning, and development for all involved. By becoming an effective mentor, you can make a meaningful contribution to the growth and advancement of your field while also gaining personal and professional fulfilment from supporting others on their journey to success. Embrace the opportunity to mentor others and pay it forward by sharing your knowledge, experiences, and expertise with the next generation of professionals in your field.

Career Mastery Exercise

1. Reflecting on Your Journey

Objective: Reflect on your personal and professional journey to identify key experiences and lessons that can be shared with a mentee.

- **Exercise:** Write a 500-word essay on a significant challenge you faced in your career and how you overcame it. Highlight the key lessons learned and how these can be valuable to your mentees.

2. Establishing Clear Goals

Objective: Define clear objectives and expectations for a mentoring relationship.

- **Exercise:** Develop a mentoring plan with your mentee. Include specific goals, a timeline for achieving them, and the steps needed to reach these goals. Schedule regular check-ins to review and adjust the plan as necessary.

3. Building Trust and Rapport

Objective: Create a supportive and trusting relationship with your mentee.

- **Exercise:** Conduct a get-to-know-you session with your mentee. Ask about their background, career aspirations, and any challenges they are currently facing. Share your own experiences to establish common ground and build rapport.

4. Providing Guidance and Support

Objective: Offer practical guidance and support based on your own experiences.

- **Exercise:** Identify a specific area where your mentee needs improvement. Provide resources, such as articles, books, or online courses, and discuss strategies to address this area. Follow up to see how they are progressing and offer additional support as needed.

5. Encouraging Self-Reflection and Growth

Objective: Encourage your mentee to reflect on their experiences and identify growth areas.

- **Exercise:** Ask your mentee to keep a journal of their experiences and reflections over a month. Schedule a meeting to discuss their entries and identify key themes and areas for further development.

6. Empowering and Encouraging

Objective: Empower your mentee to take ownership of their growth and development.

- **Exercise:** Identify a project or task that your mentee can lead independently. Provide guidance and support, but allow them to take charge. After completion, discuss what went well, what could be improved, and how the experience contributed to their growth.

7. Leading by Example

Objective: Demonstrate the behaviours and values you want to instil in your mentee.

- **Exercise:** Identify a situation where you can demonstrate a key leadership behaviour or value, such as integrity, accountability, or resilience. Invite your mentee to observe or participate, and afterwards, discuss what they learned from the experience.

8. Paying It Forward

Objective: Contribute to the growth and advancement of your field by mentoring others.

- **Exercise:** Commit to a specific action that will help pay it forward in your field, such as writing a blog post on your mentoring experiences, speaking at a conference, or starting a mentoring group in your organisation. Set a timeline for completing this action and share your progress with your mentee.

9. Evaluating the Mentoring Relationship

Objective: Evaluate the effectiveness of the mentoring relationship and identify areas for improvement.

- **Exercise:** At the end of a set period (e.g., six months), conduct a formal evaluation of the mentoring relationship with your mentee. Use a feedback form to assess what worked well, what could be improved, and how the relationship has contributed to both parties' growth. Use this feedback to enhance future mentoring efforts.

10. Expanding Your Impact

Objective: Broaden your mentoring impact by engaging with the wider community.

- **Exercise:** Participate in or organise a mentoring event, such as a workshop, panel discussion, or networking session. Encourage your mentee to get involved and share their experiences. Reflect on the impact of the event and consider ways to continue engaging with the broader community.

SIX

ADAPTABILITY AND FUTUREPROOFING

EMBRACING CHANGE

Staying Agile in a Dynamic Job Market

Introduction

The job market in today's world is rapidly changing, thus adapting to change is essential for professional success and growth. This section explores the importance of embracing change, staying agile, and thriving amidst uncertainty in your career journey.

> "Do not be afraid of change or transition. Welcome it with open arms; you never know where it could take you."

Understanding the Dynamics of Change

Change is inevitable and constant in the modern job market, driven by factors such as technological advancements, economic shifts, and globalisation. Embracing change involves recognising its inevitability, understanding its drivers and impacts, and adopting a curiosity, flexibility, and resilience mindset. Since I began my career in health and safety, I can categorically tell you that my industry has changed every year, particularly in the area of technological advancements. These are evident when I attend annual conferences and exhibitions, where I see new innovations that cut across risk assessment software, accident management systems, emergency evacuation systems, personal protective equipment, BIG data processing, artificial intelligence etc. As the world evolves, I need to understand that as a health and safety professional, the risk profile of various industries will also evolve, which means my knowledge about these risks and how to address them must also evolve. If I remain stuck in my knowledge base from five years ago, then I stand the risk of being left behind and gradually becoming unmarketable. Ask yourself certain questions about what is pertinent to your industry at every point in time to understand how you can better adapt your skillset to remain competitive in the marketplace.

Cultivating a Growth Mindset

A growth mindset is the belief that abilities and intelligence can be developed through effort, learning, and perseverance. Cultivate a growth mindset by embracing challenges, seeking opportunities for growth and learning, and viewing failures and setbacks as opportunities for improvement and development. I have mentioned earlier that the day you stop learning is the day you start dying. The reason is that learning is key to growth, and what we call death is when growth slows down or stops entirely. The issue I have observed among many professionals is this sense of comfort and security derived from staying with what you know as opposed to pushing the boundaries of your knowledge to seek more. This is why you have people who stay in toxic jobs and unfulfilling careers because of the fear of the unknown. My past experiences have corroborated the popular saying that 90% of the things I worry about end up not happening. This has been an eye-opener for me to take more risks and challenge myself constantly, with less focus on what-ifs. The same approach applies to investing in the stock market; no one knows what could happen tomorrow, but we can predict and anticipate probable outcomes based on previous trends to make informed decisions. I encourage you to embrace a mindset of consistent growth and self-development.

Adapting to New Technologies and Trends

Technological advancements and industry trends are reshaping the job market at a rapid pace. Stay abreast of new technologies, tools, and trends relevant to your field, and continuously upgrade your skills and knowledge to remain competitive and relevant in the marketplace. Embrace lifelong learning and seek out opportunities for professional development and upskilling. In earlier sections of this book, I referred to taking courses as part of my continuing professional development. These courses are not always directly related to my hard technical and professional skills but also skills related to leadership, project management, IT, people management, communication, sales, etc. According to award-winning and bestselling author Myron Golden, there are four levels of value which you can leverage for wealth creation.[32] At the lowest level of *"implementation"*, the main resources leveraged to make money are muscle and time, where professionals or skilled workers earn between minimum wage and an average of $80,000 per annum, depending on the value they provide. As you climb the ladder, the next level of *"unification"* leverages management skills, people, and time to make money. This is where you employ people skills and delegate responsibilities as a manager, with average annual earnings of around $40,000 to $250,000. At the next level of *"communication,"* the value you leverage to make money is your mouth, which could get you to where you earn $100,000 to $100 million yearly. This is where actors, musicians, script writers and songwriters (or authors) communicate in a way that moves the masses and stirs up conversations that create cashflow. The highest level of *"imagination"* is where the most wealth is made by using your mind and money as leverage to make more money. At this level, you can make anything from $1 million to trillions of dollars by thinking out ideas that can transform or revolutionise an industry sector, nation, or the world. If you get better at thinking and talking, you will make more money and be a leading voice in your industry. Remember that you do not get paid based on the difficulty of the work you do but on the level of value you deliver.

---

[32] *How To Get the Most Out Of 4 Levels of Value,* 2023, https://www.youtube.com/watch?v=_kdpDuoDjvA.

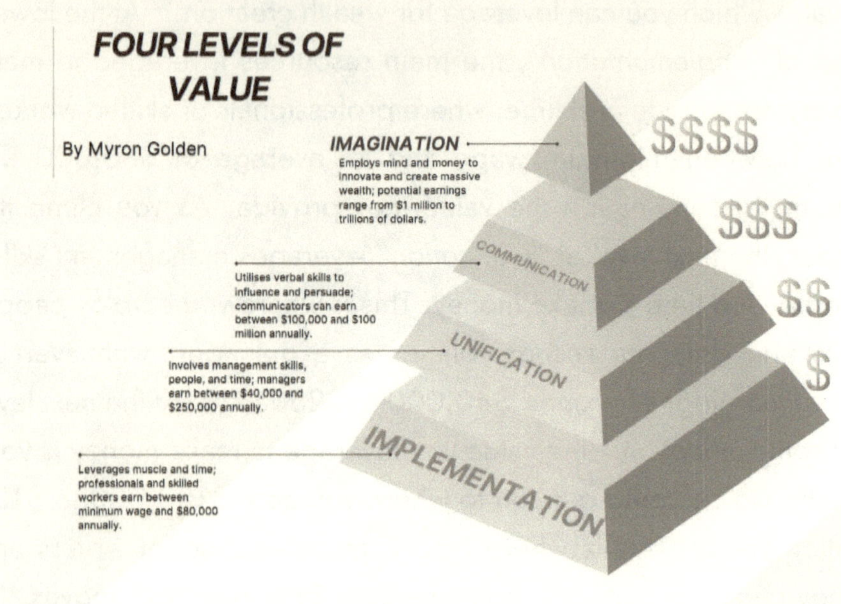

The Four Levels of Value [31]

Flexibility and Adaptability

Flexibility and adaptability are essential skills for navigating change and uncertainty in the job market. Be open to new ideas, perspectives, and ways of working, and be willing to adapt your approach and strategies in response to changing circumstances. Cultivate resilience and agility in your career by embracing change with a positive attitude and mindset. My life story tells you how much of a diverse and wide-ranging experience I have across various disciplines. When I was going through each of these phases, it seemed as though I had no end goal or was being tossed about by the waves of lacking a definite career purpose. However, in hindsight, I can attest that my experiences all culminated in giving me a well-rounded perspective as a consultant across various industry sectors today. One thing that stayed constant throughout my career journey was that I viewed every single experience I had as a learning curve and not a destination, and I still do. I am very sure that when Jeff Bezos started the Amazon bookstore in his garage or Mark Zuckerberg started Facebook in his university hostel, they never anticipated that these would become multi-billion-dollar enterprises. However, one thing that persisted in their distinctive journeys was the ability to adapt and be flexible to the demands of the changing world. Facebook and Amazon as conglomerates, which they are today, are still growing on a consistent basis from inception. It is vital to remain flexible and adaptable to the increasing demands of our rapidly changing world and do all you can to stay ahead of the game by investing in your most prized possession — your mind!

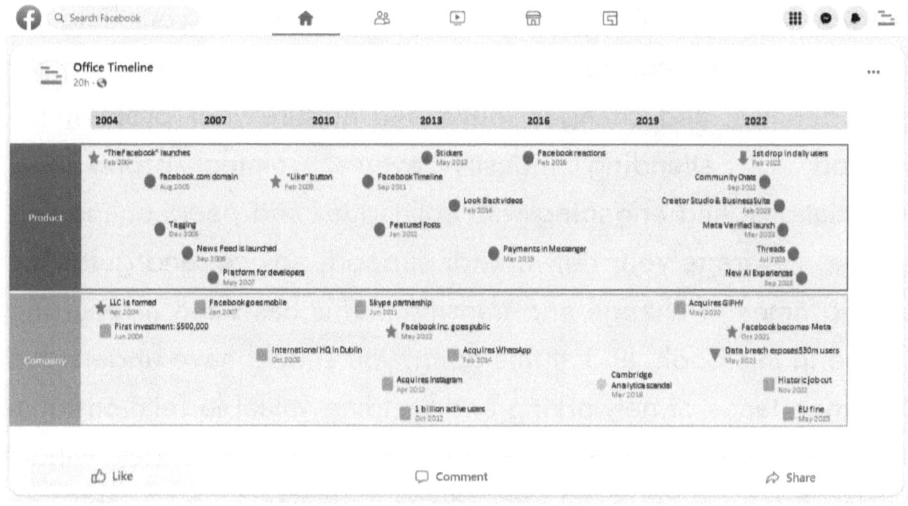

Facebook History Timeline[33]

---

[33] Tim Stumbles, 'History of Facebook Timeline', 2018, https://www.officetimeline.com/blog/facebook-history-timeline.

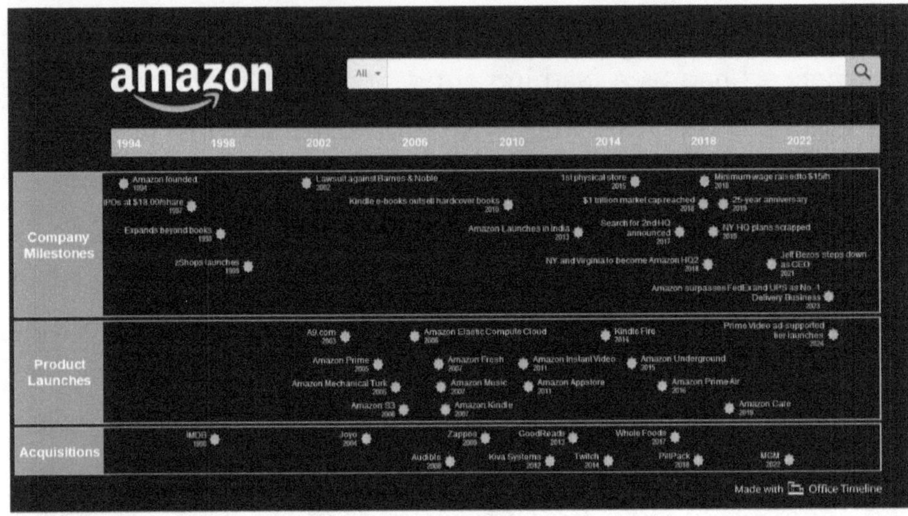

Amazon History Timeline [34]

Networking and Building Relationships

Networking and building relationships with others in your field are invaluable for staying informed about job market trends, opportunities, and changes. Build and nurture your professional network by attending industry events, joining professional associations, and engaging with colleagues and peers online and offline. Leverage your network for support, advice, and guidance during times of change and transition. This has been a recurring theme in this book, and at this point, you should have understood the importance of networking and building valuable relationships. I, for one, would not be anywhere near where I am today without leveraging on meaningful networks and relationships I established over the years of my education and professional career. I recommend you take time on an annual basis to attend conferences

---

[34] Eddy Malik, 'Amazon History Timeline', 2017,
https://www.officetimeline.com/blog/amazon-history-timeline.

related to your field of practice or networking events. You could also search out videos on the web of astute professionals in your field and drop them an email with any questions or thoughts you may have, and this could well be a good way of building that initial connection that may blossom into an amazing working relationship tomorrow.

Embracing Career Transitions

Career transitions are a natural and inevitable part of professional growth and development. Embrace career transitions as opportunities for growth, learning, and exploration rather than viewing them as setbacks or failures. Approach career transitions with a sense of curiosity, optimism, and adaptability, and be open to exploring new opportunities and possibilities that align with your interests and goals. As someone who has transitioned across multiple industry sectors, I am best positioned to give an account of how transitioning has elevated me to where I am today. When I started my academic career, I was heavily sceptical about the prospects of transitioning into industry. I had already established a solid foundation of academic repertoire, including journal publications, professional development plans, mentors, colleagues, etc. However, the transition into industry came as an unexpected change at a time when my career in academia started taking off. I remember saying to my wife that I preferred academia to industry as I felt the former would offer me a better work-life balance. I was also more established there, as opposed to sojourning on to unfamiliar territories. She said in clear terms that I was not the only determinant of what opportunity might present itself to me, and all I had to do was stay prepared. Looking back, it was the best decision I made today. I not only still lecture across multiple tertiary institutions, but also have the corresponding industry experience to leverage and boost the theoretical aspects of my career, which I have already become an expert in. Transitioning into the industry, while a daunting task at the time, became a fulfilling aspect of my journey that has enabled me to establish new connections with other industry professionals and corporate clients and collaborate with educational institutions for research and development purposes. So, I will say, do not be afraid of the transition. Welcome it with open arms; you never know where it could take you.

Resilience and Perseverance

Resilience and perseverance are essential qualities for navigating change and uncertainty in the job market. Cultivate resilience by building a strong support network, practising self-care and stress management techniques, and maintaining a positive outlook and mindset during challenging times. Persevere in the face of setbacks and obstacles and remain focused on your long-term goals and aspirations. "The best things in life don't come easy, but those things are worth the sacrifice," says Adriana Locke.[35] I have used the palm tree and skyscraper analogy to explain the importance of time variations relating to your career journey's peculiarity. It is vital not to give up easily because you are not experiencing career growth at a pace you anticipate being appropriate. Remember that

---

[35] Adriana Locke, 'Adriana Locke Quotes (Author of Crank)', 2024, https://www.goodreads.com/author/quotes/8379774.Adriana_Locke.

it takes a deeper foundation to hold a higher building and deeper roots to hold a taller tree. You must learn to work hard in silence and let your success be your noise. Sometimes, we put unnecessary pressure on ourselves by counting our eggs before they are hatched, which could deter us from achieving our dreams. When setting goals, also remember that there could be pitfalls along the way, but never fail to count these as experiences and not ultimate outcomes. Every time I have made a huge stride in my career, it has been borne out of not taking no for an answer and being resilient and perseverant to ensure I attain my goal. The same can be said of you if you are truly determined to achieve what you set your mind on, irrespective of the potholes or roadblocks you might encounter.

Summary

Embracing change is essential for staying agile and thriving in today's dynamic job market. By cultivating a growth mindset, adapting to new technologies and trends, fostering flexibility and adaptability, building relationships, embracing career transitions, and cultivating resilience and perseverance, you can confidently navigate change and emerge stronger and more resilient in your career journey. Embrace change as an opportunity for growth, learning, and exploration, and approach it with a sense of curiosity, optimism, and adaptability.

Career Mastery Exercise

Understanding the Dynamics of Change
Exercise 1: Reflecting on Change Dynamics

- **Objective:** Reflect on the dynamics of change within your industry and how you have responded to these changes.
- **Task:** Write a 300-word reflection on a significant change in your industry over the past five years. How did this change affect your role? What steps did you take to adapt?
- **Questions to Consider:**
  - What technological advancements or economic shifts have impacted your field?
  - How have these changes influenced your daily tasks or responsibilities?
  - What proactive measures did you take to stay relevant?

Cultivating a Growth Mindset
Exercise 2: Developing a Growth Mindset

- **Objective:** Develop a mindset that embraces challenges and views setbacks as opportunities for growth.
- **Task:** Set a professional development goal for the next three months. Outline the steps you will take to achieve this goal and how you will measure your progress.
- **Steps to Follow:**
  - Define a specific, measurable, achievable, relevant, and time-bound (SMART) goal.
  - Identify the resources or skills you need to achieve this goal.
  - Create a weekly plan to work towards this goal.

   o Reflect on your progress at the end of each week.

Adapting to New Technologies and Trends
Exercise 3: Staying Current with Industry Trends

- **Objective:** Stay updated on new technologies and trends relevant to your field.
- **Task:** Choose a new technology or trend that has emerged in your industry. Research its implications and write a brief report on how it could impact your work.
- **Steps to Follow:**
    - Select a recent technological advancement or trend.
    - Research its applications and potential impacts on your industry.
    - Write a 500-word report summarising your findings and suggesting how you might adapt to this trend.

Flexibility and Adaptability
Exercise 4: Embracing Flexibility

- **Objective:** Cultivate flexibility and adaptability in your professional approach.
- **Task:** Identify a recent situation where you had to adapt quickly to a change at work. Reflect on how you handled it and what you learned from the experience.
- **Questions to Consider:**
    - What was the change or challenge you faced?
    - How did you adapt your approach or strategy?
    - What were the outcomes, and what did you learn from this experience?

Networking and Building Relationships
Exercise 5: Expanding Your Network

- **Objective:** Build and nurture professional relationships within your industry.
- **Task:** Identify three industry events, conferences, or online forums that you will attend or join in the next six months. Set specific goals for what you want to achieve by participating in these events.
- **Steps to Follow:**
  - Research and list three relevant events or forums.
  - Define your goals for attending each event (e.g., meeting potential mentors, learning about new trends, networking with peers).
  - After attending each event, write a brief reflection on what you learned and how it benefited your professional network.

Embracing Career Transitions
Exercise 6: Navigating Career Transitions

- **Objective:** Embrace career transitions as opportunities for growth and development.
- **Task:** Reflect on a major career transition you have experienced or are considering. Write a plan outlining the steps you will take to manage this transition effectively.
- **Questions to Consider:**
  - What prompted the career transition?
  - What are your goals for this transition?
  - What steps will you take to ensure a smooth and successful transition?

o   How will you measure your success in this new phase of your career?

Resilience and Perseverance
Exercise 7: Building Resilience

- **Objective:** Develop resilience and perseverance in the face of professional challenges.
- **Task:** Create a personal resilience plan that includes strategies for managing stress, seeking support, and maintaining a positive outlook during challenging times.
- **Steps to Follow:**
  o   Identify your key sources of stress and how they impact you.
  o   List strategies for managing stress (e.g., exercise, mindfulness, seeking support from mentors).
  o   Set goals for maintaining a positive mindset and tracking your progress.
  o   Regularly review and update your resilience plan as needed.

FUTURE TRENDS

—·—

Anticipating Industry Shifts and Positioning Yourself for Success

Introduction

In our consistently evolving global landscape, staying ahead of industry trends is crucial for professional success and relevance. This section explores the importance of anticipating future trends, understanding industry shifts, and positioning yourself for success in a dynamic and evolving landscape.

"

"According to the second law of thermodynamics, there is no such thing as perpetual motion. Everything slows down. Everything, if left unattended, will deteriorate."

- Rudolf Clausius[36]

"

---

[36] Rudolf Clausius, 'I. on the Moving Force of Heat, and the Laws Regarding the Nature of Heat Itself Which Are Deducible Therefrom', *The London, Edinburgh, and Dublin Philosophical Magazine and Journal of Science* 2, no. 8 (1851): 1–21.

The Need for Anticipation

Anticipating future trends is essential for staying competitive and relevant in today's fast-paced world. By staying ahead of industry shifts, professionals can identify emerging opportunities, anticipate challenges, and proactively position themselves for career success. During the course of my career, I have metamorphosed into multiple variations of what I thought my goals and aspirations should look like, mostly based on the constantly changing demands of the world and how my discipline fitted around it. Have you ever done a certification course only to realise it is no longer required? Maybe you have acquired a new degree, and on completion, jobs do not seem forthcoming, and you are already considering switching career paths. You are not alone; these stories are all too familiar nowadays. One of the key reasons for this instability is that the world has gradually transitioned across multiple industrial revolutions. Therefore, to remain competitive and highly sought after, you must anticipate and set yourself up based on your industry sector's current and future transitions.

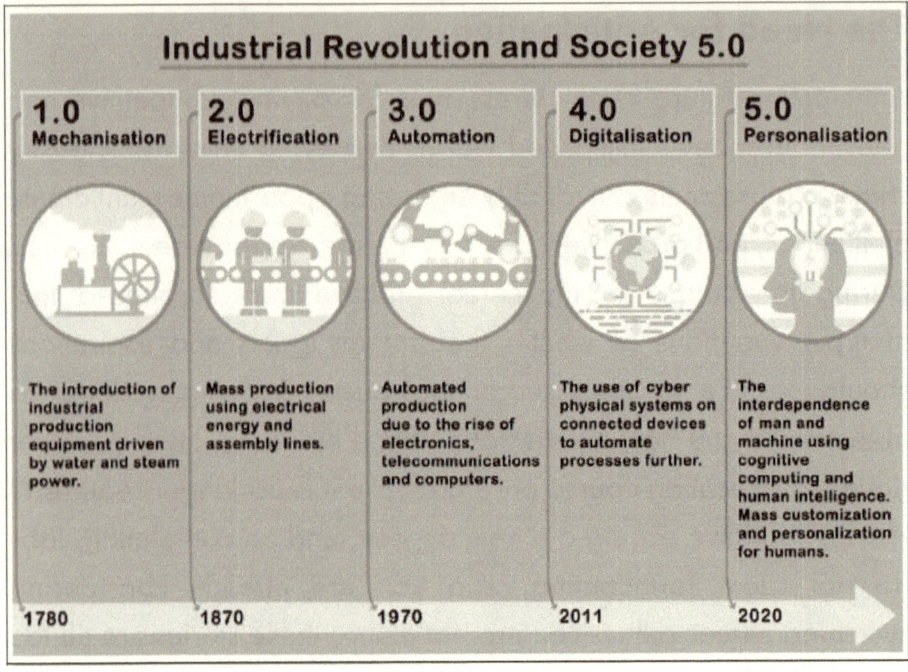

The timeline of industrial revolutions and the emergence of Industry 5.0 following the COVID-19 pandemic in 2020.[37]

Tracking Industry Trends

Stay informed about industry trends by actively monitoring news, publications, and reports related to your field. Join industry associations, attend conferences and events, and participate in online forums and discussions to stay connected with industry peers and thought leaders. Pay attention to technological advancements, regulatory changes, and shifts in consumer behaviour that may impact your industry. Whenever I attend conferences or receive monthly publications from my professional

---

[37] Zouina Sarfraz et al., 'Is COVID-19 Pushing Us to the Fifth Industrial Revolution (Society 5.0)?', *Pakistan Journal of Medical Sciences* 37 (4 January 2021), https://doi.org/10.12669/pjms.37.2.3387.

subscriptions, part of the key aspects I look out for are the trends in the industry and what is obtainable at the current time. I tend to look for existing gaps and improvements that consumers within our field are keen to see implemented. Let me take you back to when I discovered human factors as a discipline within health and safety, which currently, as illustrated in the diagram above, is a key component within Industry 5.0. When I came to study for my MSc degree in 2015 at Coventry University, one of my coursework assignments in the Health and Safety Management module hinged on analysing the human causal factors of major accidents involving contract workers in the European oil and gas industry. Prior to this time, hardly any of us knew anything about human factors as a concept. However, completing this assignment led me to identify potential gaps in existing literature, which led me to undertake a PhD programme to develop an accident human factors model for the oil and gas industry. Fast forward to my current role at the UK Health Security Agency. I am now the Human Factors Specialist for the organisation, following recommendations from the UK Health and Safety Executive (HSE) for human factors to be introduced into the organisation's processes. You can clearly see how a subject matter that seemed non-existent a few years ago suddenly has become my reality and a thriving one.

Understanding Emerging Technologies

Emerging technologies such as artificial intelligence, blockchain, and virtual reality are transforming industries and creating new opportunities for innovation and growth. Stay informed about emerging technologies relevant to your field and explore how they can be leveraged to solve problems, streamline processes, and create value for organisations and customers. In my health and safety field, which started with conceptual and theoretical models and frameworks, there is currently a massive rollout of enterprise software and IT infrastructure for health and safety management. Due to the digitalisation of processes and procedures, organisations have started ensuring that most, if not all, of their processes undergo digital transformation. If you take a quick tour of LinkedIn and other major job sites, you will discover ample job opportunities around digital transformation, software development, cloud infrastructure, etc. This is because regardless of the industry sector — healthcare, energy, education, agriculture, engineering, manufacturing, mining, etc., a constant factor remains the indispensable role of cyber-physical systems in each of these sectors — whether it be e-learning platforms in universities, remote working for organisations, computer-operated machinery for manufacturing, robotic surgeries in healthcare etc.

Adapting to Changing Consumer Preferences

Consumer preferences and behaviours constantly evolve in response to societal, economic, and technological changes. Stay attuned to changing consumer preferences, needs, and expectations, and adapt your products, services, and strategies accordingly. Embrace customer-centricity and prioritise delivering value and exceptional experiences to your target audience. This is particularly useful for business owners, especially when looking for ways to continually improve the quality of products and services you provide to customers. As a business owner, a major factor that informs my decision-making is constantly being attuned to client demands at every point in time. Sometimes, you could have this feedback in the form of direct customer reviews on your website, Google or Trustpilot reviews. However, you can also actively seek customer thoughts and perceptions by cross-benchmarking reviews of other businesses within your sector or obtaining verbal feedback once a customer has patronised your business. This helps you understand what you are doing well and what needs to improve. More importantly, it could even be a groundbreaking idea to set you up as a trailblazer in your industry. Have you ever wondered why top organisations pay for customer feedback these days? This is an avenue now for collecting valuable data and insights for consistent innovation and growth of your business. For those in the tech space, you should be familiar with the importance of user stories in incorporating certain features into a software or digital product. The same concept applies across all fields and disciplines.

Navigating Regulatory Changes

Regulatory changes and government policies can significantly impact industries and businesses. Stay informed about regulatory developments relevant to your field and ensure compliance with applicable laws and regulations. Anticipate regulatory changes and their potential implications for your organisation, and proactively adjust your strategies and operations as needed. As a basic example, you could choose to adopt theoretical frameworks such as PESTLE to examine the threats and weaknesses from political, economic, social, technological, legal and environmental factors in the external environment of your business or field. A SWOT analysis could also help you understand your key strengths, weaknesses, opportunities and threats to your business or career, which will help you develop viable solutions to address these challenges. As a health and safety professional and consultant, national regulations play a key role in my business and career, as every piece of advice I offer to clients must be based on the most up-to-date regulations. Therefore, you must lean towards future-proof solutions regarding the negative impacts of the legislation change. A good practice might be to incorporate into your organisation's risk register solutions that are not yet mandatory but advised and start looking at possible ways to implement them gradually so that it does not come as a shock if and when they become an industry requirement. For example, if you start a new business as a self-employed entity, having a health and safety policy might not be necessary as the guidance requires you to have it in place once you have five or more employees. However, you can start planning for it and putting things in place when you eventually want to upscale into a limited company.

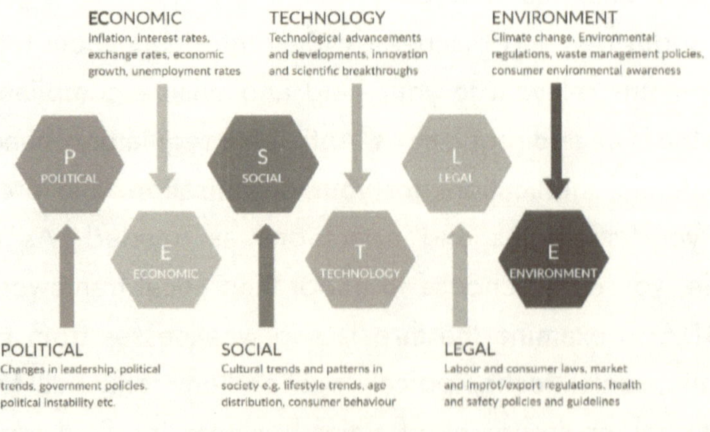

PESTLE Analysis

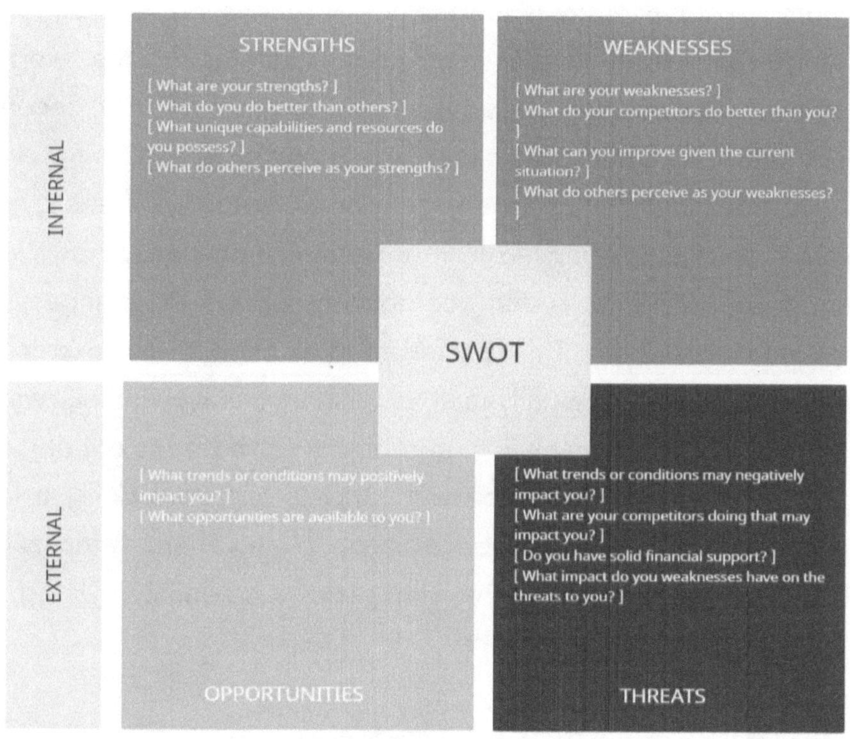

SWOT Analysis

Developing Future-Ready Skills

In today's job market that is constantly evolving, developing future-ready skills is essential for maintaining relevance and employability. Identify key skills and competencies in demand in your industry and invest in developing and honing them through training, education, and hands-on experience. Embrace lifelong learning and stay adaptable and open to acquiring new skills and knowledge throughout your career. I have repeatedly touched on the need for you to cultivate a mindset of continuous growth and development, as this sets you apart from being ordinary and extraordinary. Necessity is the mother of innovation, and so long as there continues to be emerging problems in the world, innovative solutions will be required to address them. The second law of thermodynamics states that, within any system, nothing ever remains the same [35]. Change is constant. Obviously, if energy or matter is added or removed from a system, it changes. However, even if we leave a system completely alone, it changes; it deteriorates over time. This is referred to as entropy. For example, ice in a cooler will eventually melt, a wristwatch will eventually wind down and stop, your car will stop running when it runs out of gas, streets will eventually deteriorate to gravel, and your skills, if left unattended, will eventually become obsolete. There is no such thing as perpetual motion. Everything slows down. Everything, if left unattended, will deteriorate.

Networking and Building Relationships

Networking and building relationships with others in your industry are invaluable for staying informed about industry trends, opportunities, and changes. Build and nurture your professional network by attending industry events, joining professional associations, and engaging with colleagues and peers online and offline. Leverage your network for support, advice, and guidance in navigating industry shifts and positioning yourself for success. I remember receiving an award of recognition from the Deputy Director of Health and Safety at the UK Health Security Agency. I was recommended for this award by my line manager for multiple reasons, such as my level of impact within the organisation, the detailed insight I brought into projects, and most notably, how inclusive I was in my professional practice. My ability to integrate well into a dynamic team and manage multiple relationships in all spheres within the organisation earned me much respect among my colleagues, mentees, and mentors. Thus, this led to me being recognised and awarded accordingly. However, note that some key factors in play here are things I have mentioned throughout this book — mentors, networking, relationships, excellence, innovation, etc. You must cherish and honour your personal and working relationships to go far in your career journey, and that comes from not just having outstanding people skills but also prioritising excellence in all you do and are involved in.

Summary

Anticipating future trends and industry shifts is essential for staying competitive, relevant, and successful in today's dynamic and evolving landscape. By actively tracking industry trends, understanding emerging technologies, adapting to changing consumer preferences, navigating regulatory changes, developing future-ready skills, and building relationships with industry peers, professionals can position themselves for success and thrive in their careers. Embrace change as an opportunity for growth and innovation, and proactively position yourself to capitalise on emerging opportunities and navigate challenges with confidence and resilience.

Career Mastery Exercise

1. Anticipating Future Trends

- **Reflection:** Consider the last time you encountered a significant industry shift. How did you respond? Were you prepared, or did the change catch you off guard?
- **Action:** Identify three emerging trends in your industry. Research how these trends might impact your current role and think of ways to adapt your skills or strategies to stay ahead.

2. Tracking Industry Trends

- **Reflection:** How do you currently stay informed about industry trends? Are there any sources or methods you haven't explored yet?
- **Action:** Subscribe to at least two industry-specific publications or newsletters. Commit to attending one industry event or webinar in the next three months to broaden your understanding of current trends.

3. Understanding Emerging Technologies

- **Reflection:** Think about a recent technological advancement in your field. Did you embrace it, or were you hesitant? What could you have done differently?
- **Action:** Choose one emerging technology relevant to your field. Dedicate time each week to learning about it, whether through online courses, articles, or hands-on experience.

4. Adapting to Changing Consumer Preferences

- **Reflection:** Reflect on a time when you had to adjust your product or service to meet changing consumer demands. What was the outcome?
- **Action:** Gather feedback from your clients or customers about your current offerings. Identify at least one area for improvement and create a plan to address it.

5. Navigating Regulatory Changes

- **Reflection:** How have regulatory changes impacted your work in the past? Were you proactive or reactive in dealing with these changes?
- **Action:** Conduct a PESTLE analysis for your industry, focusing on potential regulatory changes. Identify one area where you can start future-proofing your operations or strategies.

6. Developing Future-Ready Skills

- **Reflection:** Assess your current skill set. Are there any skills that are becoming obsolete? What new skills could help you stay relevant?
- **Action:** Enrol in a course or workshop that focuses on a skill relevant to the future of your industry. Set a goal to complete this training within the next six months.

7. Networking and Building Relationships

- **Reflection:** Reflect on the strength of your current professional network. Are there gaps that need to be filled?

- **Action:** Reach out to three professionals in your industry whom you haven't connected with in a while. Attend a networking event or join a professional association to expand your network.

8. Celebrating Milestones

- **Reflection:** Think about your recent achievements. Did you take the time to celebrate them? How did that affect your motivation?
- **Action:** Set a milestone or goal for the next quarter. Plan a small celebration or reward for yourself once you achieve it.

CONTINUOUS INNOVATION

*Fostering Creativity and Adaptation
in Your Career Journey*

Introduction

Innovation is not just reserved for products and services; it's also vital for personal and professional growth. This section highlights the significance of continuous innovation, fostering creativity, and adaptability throughout your career journey to thrive in a rapidly evolving world.

> "The challenge is that the day before something is truly a breakthrough, it's a crazy idea. And crazy ideas are very risky to attempt."
>
> **- Peter Diamandis**[38]

---

[38] Peter H Diamandis and Steven Kotler, *Bold: How to Go Big, Create Wealth and Impact the World* (Simon and Schuster, 2015).

Embracing a Culture of Innovation

Innovation thrives in environments that foster creativity, curiosity, and experimentation. Cultivate a culture of innovation by encouraging openness to new ideas, celebrating experimentation, and embracing failure as a natural part of the learning process. Create spaces where employees feel empowered to think outside the box, challenge the status quo, and pursue novel solutions to complex problems. One of my ardent traits, which has led me to this point in my career, has stemmed from my ability to come up with innovative solutions when confronted with problems. Sometimes, it starts with a random idea about a new concept, a different way of doing things, or a tiny tweak to an already established approach. I remember working as a Health and Safety Consultant for a client. I thought for a second that having an all-in-one health and safety software might make sense — something like Microsoft Office 365, which could house several health and safety management modules such as accident investigation, risk assessment, training, asset management, chemical inventory, etc. Fast forward to a few years down the line, this software is now being developed and rolled out by various companies and has proved to be a game changer in the industry. My point is you must learn to think on your feet and put on different lenses that help you spot problems where others don't because your breakthrough moment lies there.

Staying Curious and Seeking Inspiration

Maintain a curious mindset by seeking new experiences, ideas, and perspectives. Stay informed about industry trends, emerging technologies, and best practices through reading, attending conferences, and engaging with thought leaders in your field. Draw inspiration from diverse sources, including art, literature, science, and nature, to spark creativity and innovation in your work. My theoretical perspective in academia as a social constructivist has helped me naturally adopt a continuous interaction and feedback loop mindset with most professionals I engage with. Whenever I have discussions with someone in any field, I am keenly looking for what I can benchmark from their practice and apply to my field. A good example is when I spoke to Project Managers, Agile Coaches, Product Owners, Scrum Masters, and Business Analysts. I realised quickly that so long as you manage a set of interrelated activities with a start and end date to complete them to a specific quality or standard, at a given cost, and within a specified timeframe, you need project management skills. Following our conversations, I also observed that while the Project Managers mostly adopted traditional approaches to undertaking projects (e.g. Waterfall methodology), the latter professionals adopted more of an agile approach to their projects, most of which were in the IT and Tech sectors. I examined each approach and clearly saw the advantages and drawbacks of each and where their benefits can be greatly realised. This helped me leverage these approaches when developing systems of work, as well as standard operating procedures for my organisation and business, and adapt my practices to any projects I manage. I even undertook a few certification courses in these fields to broaden my knowledge base around managing projects across various industry sectors.

Encouraging Creative Problem-Solving

Creativity is essential for solving complex problems and driving innovation in the workplace. Encourage creative problem-solving by providing employees autonomy, support, and resources to explore new ideas and approaches. Foster interdisciplinary collaboration and diversity of thought to generate innovative solutions that challenge conventional wisdom and drive meaningful change. One of the ways I have empowered my staff to embrace creative problem-solving is by eradicating "blame culture" and, instead, instilling a culture of learning from experiences and operating an open-door policy. When employees feel that their voices are heard and their opinions will not be downplayed, it gives them the confidence to come up with crazy ideas. Just like the popular quote by Peter Diamandis, "The challenge is that the day before something is truly a breakthrough, it's a crazy idea. And crazy ideas are very risky to attempt." I always let my employees and colleagues know that no question is a stupid one, and the only stupid question is the one that is never asked. Think about it; who would have sat down to devise mathematical formulae, chemical equations, philosophical theories, various forms of artistry, etc., if they did not have a crazy idea? Encourage thinking outside the box, as the box did not always exist.

Adapting to Change and Embracing Uncertainty

The world around us is rapidly evolving, thus adaptability is key to staying relevant and resilient in your career journey. Embrace uncertainty as an opportunity for growth and innovation rather than a threat to stability and security. Develop a mindset of agility and flexibility, and be willing to pivot, iterate, and experiment in response to changing circumstances and opportunities. In previous years, I was usually anxious about the uncertainty of not knowing what tomorrow holds. I would rather plan to the very last detail with absolute certainty of the outcome, which, if I fail to achieve, will leave me with utter disappointment. However, I learned something about life after a while – we live in a flawed world where outcomes can only be predicted without absolute certainty but probability. I realised that if I truly wanted to live a happy and fulfilled life, I do not have to always seek perfection, as nothing exists in our sphere. Haruki Murakami said, "All of us are imperfect beings living in an imperfect world."[39] Therefore, we should position ourselves so that when what I call the expected unexpected comes around, we are well prepared to navigate our way through it. It is important to adopt an agile mindset of constant change, adaptation, and iteration to futureproof your skills, cope with any eventualities, and develop innovative solutions in the face of rising challenges.

Iterative Improvement and Learning from Failure

Continuous innovation involves a process of iterative improvement and learning from failure. Embrace a mindset of experimentation and iteration, where failures are seen as valuable learning experiences that inform future success. Encourage a culture of reflection and feedback, empowering individuals to experiment, take risks, and learn from successes and setbacks. Many of us harbour the desire for perfection, whether striving for top exam

---

[39] Haruki Murakami, 'A Quote from Norwegian Wood', 2024, https://www.goodreads.com/quotes/621244-all-of-us-are-imperfect-human-beings-living-in-an.

scores or aiming to lead flawless lives. This inclination stems from our innate drive for improvement. However, in a world of imperfections, expecting flawless outcomes is unrealistic. Rather than viewing this reality as disheartening, I see it as liberating. Embracing our imperfections and recognising their role in our pursuit of happiness is what truly defines contentment. According to J.K. Rowling, "it is impossible to live without failing at something unless you live so cautiously that you might as well not have lived at all, in which case you have failed by default."

Fostering Innovation in Leadership

Leaders play a critical role in fostering innovation within organisations by setting a vision, creating a supportive environment, and empowering employees to unleash their creativity and potential. Lead by example by embracing innovation, taking calculated risks, and championing a culture of experimentation and continuous learning. Provide resources, support, and recognition for innovative initiatives and celebrate successes to reinforce a culture of innovation and creativity. As a leader, I always ensure that innovation and creativity stem from the top and are part of the fabric of the overall culture of my organisation. As you must have realised by now, the tagline for my company, Nancheez Ltd, reads, *"Transforming lives by providing world-class solutions."* This means that at the heart of everything we do as a business, for every client we have, each project we undertake, and any idea we come up with, our service must be embedded in creativity and innovation. Also, this mantra indicates the importance of providing solutions as an avenue for positive transformation across various industry sectors. When staff see that you are not afraid to take risks, fail, and learn, they are encouraged not only to bring diverse ideas to the table but also to buy into the mission and vision of your organisation.

Summary

Continuous innovation is essential for personal and professional growth, driving creativity, adaptation, and resilience in today's rapidly changing world. By fostering a culture of innovation, staying curious and seeking inspiration, encouraging creative problem-solving, adapting to change, embracing uncertainty, iterating and learning from failure, and fostering innovation in leadership, individuals can unleash their full potential and thrive in their career journey. Embrace innovation as a mindset and a way of life and leverage it as a powerful tool for driving positive change and making meaningful contributions to your field and the world.

Career Mastery Exercise

Embracing a Culture of Innovation

- **Reflect:** Think about a recent challenge you faced at work. Did you come up with any innovative solutions? How did you encourage creativity within your team?
- **Action:** Identify one area in your current role where you can introduce a new, creative approach. Plan and implement this idea over the next month, and observe the outcomes.
- **Action:** Create a list of three ways you can foster a culture of innovation in your workplace. Share these ideas with your team and implement at least one.

Staying Curious and Seeking Inspiration

- **Reflect:** Recall the last time you learned something new that significantly impacted your work. How did it inspire you?
- **Action:** Set aside 30 minutes each week to explore new trends and advancements in your field. Subscribe to relevant industry newsletters or journals.
- **Action:** Attend at least one industry conference or workshop in the next six months. Network with peers and seek out new ideas and perspectives.

Encouraging Creative Problem-Solving

- **Reflect:** Consider a problem you solved recently. How did you approach it creatively? What was the outcome?
- **Action:** Schedule a brainstorming session with your team to tackle a current challenge. Encourage wild ideas and record all suggestions without judgment.
- **Action:** Implement a "no blame" culture in your workplace. Encourage open discussions about failures and what can be learned from them.

Adapting to Change and Embracing Uncertainty

- **Reflect:** Think about a recent change in your workplace. How did you adapt? What did you learn from the experience?
- **Action:** Identify a change you anticipate in your industry. Develop a plan outlining how you will adapt to this change, including any skills or knowledge you need to acquire.
- **Action:** Practise flexibility by taking on a new role or responsibility outside your comfort zone. Reflect on the experience and what you learned from it.

Iterative Improvement and Learning from Failure

- **Reflect:** Reflect on a recent failure. What did you learn from it? How did it influence your subsequent actions?
- **Action:** Adopt an iterative approach to a current project. Set short-term goals, review progress regularly, and make adjustments as needed.
- **Action:** Create a failure log where you record and reflect on failures and the lessons learned. Review this log periodically to identify patterns and areas for improvement.

Fostering Innovation in Leadership

- **Reflect:** Evaluate your current leadership style. How do you encourage innovation and creativity in your team?
- **Action:** Set up a system for recognising and rewarding innovative ideas within your team. Celebrate successes, no matter how small.
- **Action:** Lead by example. Take a calculated risk on a new project or idea and involve your team in the process. Share both the successes and lessons learned.

CHAPTER SEVEN

ACHIEVING MASTERY

THE JOURNEY CONTINUES

— · —

*Embracing Growth and Lifelong
Learning as a Master in Your Field*

Introduction

Becoming a master in your field is not the end of the journey; it's just the beginning of a lifelong pursuit of growth and learning. This section explores the importance of embracing continuous growth and lifelong learning as a master in your field.

> "In learning you will teach, and in teaching you will learn."
>
> **- Phil Collins**

The Evolution of Mastery

Mastery is not a destination but a journey of continuous growth and development. As a master in your field, you have achieved high expertise and proficiency, but the journey does not end there. Embrace the mindset of a lifelong learner, recognising that there is always more to learn, discover, and explore. Sometimes, I may come across as being ungrateful and never content with where I am or what I have achieved, but the reality is I am hardly ever satisfied with any level I find myself. Immediately I achieve something great, my next thought is, what is next? I hardly give myself any time to settle into party mode, which can sometimes be quite daunting, as I find it hard to dial out of work mode. While this can pose a challenge sometimes, especially as I have a family and other areas of my life to manage, it keeps me hungry and longing for more, leading to me doing more things that will spur my growth and development. The key here is balance — I recommend always taking time out to celebrate your wins, but also let that be a way to encourage yourself to do something that will lead to you celebrating even more in the future. That way, you stay grounded while pursuing your goals and have some time off to recharge and go again.

Staying Ahead of the Curve

It is vital to note that staying ahead of the curve in today's global marketplace requires a commitment to ongoing learning and adaptation. Keep abreast of industry trends, emerging technologies, and best practices through reading, attending conferences, and engaging with thought leaders in your field.

Invest in professional development opportunities like courses, workshops, and certifications to stay current and relevant in your industry. Whether it is related to my industry or not, I watch and read almost everything. Most of the time, when I meet someone for the first time or converse with a stranger, I find that I know something about whatever topic we are discussing. It is not because I am an expert in every field by any stretch of the imagination, but because I am like a blank canvas, or should I say a sponge that takes on every piece of information and then filters out what makes meaningful sense to me. As a Christian, for example, I still get to read other books like the Jewish Kabballah, Quran, and other religious books alongside the Bible as they offer me a panoramic worldview, contextual background, and insight into the perspectives of others. This does not mean that I get to change my religion, but it gives me additional information I need to understand my own religion and how it aligns within the broader context of others. The same approach applies to my career aspirations — I binge-watch videos on computer programming, DIY, biology, chemistry, history, politics, sports, lifestyle, religion, etc., all while maintaining my technical expertise in health and safety. I observe that this keeps me current with emerging trends across various sectors and what that means for me and my professional practice. Using a basic PESTLE analysis, remember that every business or discipline is influenced by political, economic, social, technological, legal, and environmental factors; hence, staying widely read and knowledgeable in as many areas as possible is important.

Exploring New Frontiers

As a master in your field, you have the expertise and experience to explore new frontiers and push the boundaries of what's possible. Embrace opportunities to innovate, experiment, and take calculated risks in pursuit of new ideas and breakthroughs. Cultivate a sense of curiosity and wonder and be open to exploring interdisciplinary connections and unconventional problem-solving approaches. I have said earlier that for you to build something that can be truly groundbreaking and transformational, you must think outside the box. You need to be able to question almost everything and see how things can be improved. When I came to the UK in 2015 for my MSc, I remember one of the keywords that was consistently drummed into my ears: "critical thinking". At the time, I hardly understood what it meant, but as time went on, I gradually realised that every novel contribution to the body of existing knowledge that leads to innovation is first conceived through critical thinking. As a critical thinker, when you read a book, watch a video or listen to a conversation, the thoughts constantly running through your mind should be what if, how about, however, maybe, possibly, etc. You should always be willing to explore other possibilities despite glaring facts and strong opinions. When you do this, you can tease out some sound arguments which could revolutionise your industry, field, or sector.

Mentoring and passing on the Torch

When you obtain mastery in your area of expertise, also remember that you are responsible for mentoring and inspiring the next generation of professionals. Share your knowledge, experiences, and insights with others through mentoring, coaching, and teaching. Invest in the growth and development of others and empower them to reach their full potential and make their own contributions to the field. One of the compelling reasons why I decided to write this book was to not let all I have experienced go to waste without it helping someone out there. I have been through a lot in my life, career-wise, especially as an international student who came to the UK and is now established in my field as a recognised published author, practitioner, and consultant. As I pointed out earlier, I have received mentorship requests from not just people at work who are inspired by the quality of my process and outputs, but also individuals who find themselves in some parts of my story. I asked my wife a question on a particular day, "What would you say I am good at"? Her response was quite profound, "I will say you are good at helping people become better by providing solutions for them." As vague as it must have sounded on first hearing, I had to ponder over that response for a while and took some time to reflect on my life trajectory to date. It was then I realised that what brings me the most fulfilment in life is exactly what she said. When I see someone who has come to me confused about something but leaves after our conversation with some level of assuredness and certainty, it fills me with utmost satisfaction that I am contributing to this planet one person at a time. Honestly, I will encourage you to take some people with you as you advance the career ladder. In the words of Phil Collins, "In learning you will teach, and in teaching you will learn."[40]

---

[40] Collins, 'A Quote by Phil Collins', 2024, https://www.goodreads.com/quotes/32942-in-learning-you-will-teach-and-in-teaching-you-will.

Giving Back to the Community

Contributing to the community is essential to being a master in your field. Give back to your profession by volunteering, serving on committees, and participating in industry associations and organisations. Share your time, expertise, and resources to support initiatives that advance the field and benefit society. I currently hold a voluntary leadership position in my church as one of the professionals heading the Academic Unit. This department was set up to assist students who, just like myself, came into the country to study without an exact knowledge of how the educational system in the UK works. I have developed and delivered sessions for these students around Scholarly Research, Plagiarism, Referencing, Critical Thinking, Academic Writing, Dissertation, Research Methods and Design, Data Analysis, and Academic Development. Upon delivery of these sessions, my team and I discovered that students who initially had little or no understanding of these concepts left the sessions feeling more confident and empowered. Better still, most of them come out with excellent grades and become astute professionals in their chosen fields. The sense of pride and accomplishment that comes with this is second to none, as you clearly see how impactful your contributions can be. The best part is that it is something borne out of a sheer desire to make a difference and not because you are getting paid for it, again giving you that sense of fulfilment and responsibility.

Maintaining Balance and Well-being

As you continue your journey of growth and learning, remember to prioritise balance and well-being. Take time for self-care, relaxation, and rejuvenation to prevent burnout and maintain your physical, emotional, and mental health. Cultivate a sense of gratitude and fulfilment and find joy and meaning in both your professional and personal pursuits. As I said earlier, there is nothing wrong with being driven and constantly chasing your goals and dreams. However, sometimes, you should give yourself a pat on the back and appreciate your phenomenal work. If that means going on a well-deserved holiday, spending time with family, doing your favourite hobbies, etc., just do what makes you happy and feel rewarded. Remember that a vehicle also needs routine servicing and MOT to keep running in its best condition. The same applies to you — pause, refill, reset and restart. Compile all your notable achievements into a folder or portfolio as something to refuel you on the days you might feel a little demotivated. Remember, there is no one like you; you did this, and you deserve the best!

Summary

The journey of mastery is a lifelong pursuit of growth, learning, and contribution. Embrace the opportunity to continue growing and evolving as a master in your field, and commit to lifelong learning, exploration, and innovation. Share your knowledge, mentor others, give back to the community, and prioritise balance and well-being as you continue to make your mark on the world. Remember that mastery is not a destination but a journey, and the adventure continues as long as you remain open to growth and discovery.

Career Mastery Exercise

Reflection and Action Plan: The Journey Continues: Embracing Growth and Lifelong Learning as a Master in Your Field

Embracing a Culture of Innovation

- **Reflect:** What innovative ideas have you implemented recently in your professional practice? How did these ideas impact your work or organisation?
- **Action:** Identify one new area in your field that interests you. Research recent developments in this area and consider how you might incorporate these innovations into your work.

Staying Ahead of the Curve

- **Reflect:** How do you currently stay informed about industry trends and emerging technologies? Are there any gaps in your knowledge?
- **Action:** Commit to reading at least one industry-related article or paper each week. Join relevant online forums or professional groups to stay connected with thought leaders.

Exploring New Frontiers

- **Reflect:** When was the last time you took a calculated risk in your career? What was the outcome, and what did you learn from the experience?
- **Action:** Choose a project or idea that pushes the boundaries of your current expertise. Develop a plan to

explore and implement this project, keeping track of your progress and lessons learned.

Mentoring and Passing on the Torch

- **Reflect:** Think about a time when you mentored someone. What impact did it have on their growth and your development?
- **Action:** Identify one individual in your professional network who could benefit from your mentorship. Reach out to offer guidance and support, and set regular check-ins to track their progress.

Giving Back to the Community

- **Reflect:** How have you contributed to your professional community in the past year? Are there additional ways you could give back?
- **Action:** Volunteer for a committee, industry association, or local organisation related to your field. Share your expertise through presentations, articles, or workshops.

Maintaining Balance and Well-being

- **Reflect:** How do you currently balance your professional growth with personal well-being? Are there areas where you could improve?
- **Action:** Schedule regular self-care activities, such as exercise, meditation, or hobbies, into your weekly routine. Set boundaries to ensure you have time for relaxation and rejuvenation.

GIVING BACK

*Contributing to Your Community
and Leaving a Lasting Legacy*

Introduction

While achieving personal success is rewarding, contributing to the betterment of society is equally fulfilling. This section explores the significance of giving back, contributing to your community, and leaving a lasting legacy beyond your professional achievements.

> *"We make a living by what we get, but we make a life by what we give."*
>
> **- Winston Churchill**

Understanding the Power of Giving Back

Giving back involves using your time, resources, and talents to positively impact others and the community. It is rooted in empathy, compassion, and a desire to create positive change in the world. By giving back, individuals have the opportunity to make a difference, foster connections, and leave a lasting legacy that extends beyond their lifetime. I always advise my mentees when they design their long-term visions and goals to ponder on what exactly they are trying to solve on a global scale. How do their visions align with creating a lasting positive impact on Earth, and how can they make this a reality? The truth is not everyone; in fact, only a handful of people will end up being known on a global scale. However, if we set our sights on how our visions can transform the world, implementing this dream starts within ourselves. Then, it extends to our direct communities, our states or provinces, the nation and continent, and the world at large. Wherever we get to in our journey of creating this long-lasting impact, if we set things in motion on the right foundation, someone tomorrow can carry on from where we stopped and finish that legacy we started on the right footing. We look at Steve Jobs, who founded Apple in 1976 and passed away in 2011, but he has left a legacy behind as one of the world's most valuable and transformational companies. Walt Disney passed away in 1966; however, the company continued to expand and thrive after his death, becoming a global entertainment powerhouse. Henry Ford founded the Ford Motor Company in 1903 and played a key role in its early success. He passed away in 1947, but the company continued to grow and innovate, becoming one of the largest automobile manufacturers in the world. Louis Vuitton founded his luxury brand in 1854, and after his death in 1892, the brand continued to expand and evolve, becoming synonymous with high-end fashion and luxury goods. These examples demonstrate how businesses can continue to thrive and grow even after the passing of their founders, often building upon the foundation laid by their visionary leaders.

Identifying Ways to Contribute

Depending on your interests, skills, and resources, there are countless ways to give back and contribute to your community. Volunteer your time with local nonprofits, charities, or community organisations that align with your values and passions. Donate money, goods, or services to causes that are meaningful to you. Use your expertise and influence to advocate for social justice, environmental sustainability, or other important issues. I believe everyone has something to offer; however, the key lies in identifying what and how to offer what you have. For every single experience you have encountered in life, there is someone out there who can reap immense benefits from it. In fact, your failures are more valuable than your successes because they teach others what to avoid on their own journeys. This is one reason why I am not scared to share my failures with my mentees. I view success and failure as learning curves and not outcomes. I have made several contributions in my own little way in my career path through my PhD research, journal publications, this book, mentorship schemes, seminars, workshops, etc. I have also identified more ways to contribute my own quota to the world, especially through digital platforms such as YouTube, Instagram, Facebook, etc., to reach a wider community predominantly made up of future generations. As my business continually expands across industry and geographical boundaries, my contribution will also focus on not just job creation or providing business-to-business (B2B) solutions, but also raising professionals who can go out and replicate the excellence they have acquired from being associated with me. This is bolstered by the Biblical principle of being fruitful, multiplying, replenishing, subduing, and having dominion over your industry, geographical location or wherever you find yourself.

Mentoring and Supporting Others

Mentoring and supporting others is a powerful way to give back and positively impact individuals' lives. Share your knowledge, experiences, and insights with others through mentoring, coaching, or teaching. Empower and uplift others by providing guidance, encouragement, and support to help them reach their full potential and achieve their goals. I wish to share a few quotes from Mentor Resources in this section because I believe each of them will relate to someone out there.[41]

---

[41] Kim Wise, '20 Inspiring Mentoring Quotes', 2020,
https://www.mentorresources.com/mentoring-blog/20-inspiring-mentoring-quotes.

"

"Our chief want in life is somebody who will make us do what we can."

— Ralph Waldo Emerson

"My job is not to be easy on people. My job is to take these great people we have and to push them and make them even better."

— Steve Jobs

"We make a living by what we get, but we make a life by what we give."

— Winston Churchill

"The delicate balance of mentoring someone is not creating them in your own image but giving them the opportunity to create themselves."

— Steven Spielberg

"The mind is not a vessel that needs filling, but wood that needs igniting."

— Plutarch

"We're here for a reason. I believe a bit of the reason is to throw little torches out to lead people through the dark."

— Whoopi Goldberg

"If I have seen further, it is by standing on the shoulders of giants."

— Isaac Newton

"You cannot teach a man anything. You can only help him discover it within himself"

— Galileo Galilei

"Show me a successful individual, and I'll show you someone who had real positive influences in his or her life. I don't care what you do for a living—if you do it well, I'm sure there was someone cheering you on or showing you the way. A mentor."

— Denzel Washington

"A mentor is someone who sees more talent and ability within you than you see in yourself and helps bring it out of you."

— Bob Proctor

"If you cannot see where you are going, ask someone who has been there before."

— J Loren Norris

"Mentoring is a brain to pick, an ear to listen, and a push in the right direction."

— John Crosby

"A mentor is someone who sees more talent and ability within you than you see in yourself and helps bring it out of you."

— Bob Proctor

"A mentor is someone who allows you to see the hope inside yourself."

— Oprah Winfrey

"

Creating Sustainable Change

Creating sustainable change requires a long-term commitment to addressing root causes and systemic issues within communities. Collaborate with others to identify community needs and develop solutions promoting equity, justice, and opportunity. Advocate for policies and initiatives that address social, economic, and environmental challenges and create positive change at the systemic level. Most business professionals would love to look at the PESTLE analysis as a business environment tool that helps you identify threats and weaknesses used in a SWOT analysis. However, I have referred to this tool repetitively in this book to convey certain points, especially those related to identifying ways to keep your skills future-proof as a professional. The reason for this is that most policies made by governments and industries are not made without some level of PESTLE analysis being carried out. Whether it be a new government, new economic policy, emerging social construct, technological advancement, enactment or amendment of legislation, or environmental policies, we as professionals need to ensure that we take these factors into cognisance to map out adaptable, flexible, and sustainable strategies for how our legacies will be built regardless of any change introduced by these factors. For example, if you are an automobile expert, how does a change in government influence the kind of cars you manufacture or procure over the next decade? Does the current cost of living crisis and interest rate hikes imply that there might be reduced accessibility to car loans and finances for a larger percentage of the population? Are more people leaning now towards electric/hybrid vehicles, or are fossil fuel engines still projected to be viable in the future? Are there new and emerging car technologies you must have as part of your fleet? Depending on where you are located, do the environmental legislations, e.g. Ultra Low Emission Zones (ULEZ), have any implications for future car sales? Does a change in legislation about certain manufacturing standards affect your brand and what you stand for? Regardless of your sector, these are all questions you should ask when ascertaining ways to create sustainable change.

Leaving a Lasting Legacy

Leaving a lasting legacy is about making a meaningful and enduring impact that transcends generations. Consider how you can use your time, talents, and resources to leave a positive legacy in your community and beyond. Whether through philanthropy, volunteerism, advocacy, or innovation, strive to create a legacy that inspires and empowers others to continue making the world better. I always ask myself a question, especially regarding my career — when I am done, what next? How does what I have done and achieved impact the next generations? Will I be known as someone who paved the way for something greater to be birthed? These questions are imperative when designing your long-term visions because your career should create something that will outlast you. We talk about several individuals today — inventors, philosophers, monarchs, politicians, activists, etc.- mainly because of the value of what they have contributed during their time, which makes them relevant across several generations. This brings a movie to mind — Troy — where Achilles was told by his mother, the goddess Thetis, that if he did not go to war, he would live a happy life, but his legacy would be forgotten. However, if he went to battle, he would die but be remembered eternally.[42]

> "Mother tells me,
> the immortal goddess Thetis with her glistening feet,
> that two fates bear me on to the day of death.
> If I hold out here and lay siege to Troy,
> my journey home is gone, but my glory never dies.
> If I voyage back to the fatherland I love,
> my pride, my glory dies. . .."
>
> **- Achilles, the Iliad IX, 500-506**

Achilles opted to die in battle but be remembered for multiple generations, rather than live a happy, comfortable life and never be remembered. Even Jesus himself lived for only thirty-three years[43] — which would be considered a short life in those times, never mind today — of which he did His ministry for only three years from age thirty; however, his legacy is the greatest ever created. Let this leave a constant reminder that we all have a maximum of a hundred years or a little above that to live on earth, but what we do while we are here determines how well we lived our lives.

---

[42] Patrick Garvey, 'Making Sense of a Hero's Motivation', Ancient Heroes, 2015, http://ancientheroes.net/blog/reconsidering-a-heros-motivation.
[43] Bible, *King James Bible*.

Celebrating the Impact of Giving Back

Celebrate the impact of giving back and recognise the contributions of individuals and organisations making a difference in their communities. Share impact stories and inspiration to inspire others to get involved and give back. Cultivate a culture of generosity, empathy, and compassion that encourages everyone to play a part in creating a better world for future generations. I must point out here that a thin line exists between chasing clout and inspiring others to create impact. The distinction is in the motive driving each decision; if you are more concerned about what is in it, your driving factor is clout chasing. However, if you are more focused on the bigger picture of creating a lasting legacy that will improve the world one way or the other, then you have the right motivational factor. There is nothing wrong with desiring positive outcomes for your business or career; however, that should not be the ultimate desire. Instead, that should come as a by-product of the value you provide to your industry or community as a professional. Some people might give money to a cause to become well-known, while others might do the same because that is an inherent value they stand for. When you pursue value, success pursues you in return. The price of a thing is determined by how much value has been communicated to the buyer by the seller. This could be your salary, product, service, brand, etc. People will only pay for how much they perceive your product or service to be, primarily communicated by what you represent — your brand. This is why, regardless of the quality of leather used to make a luxury bag, a Louis Vuitton bag will always be priced more than a high street bag. What separates their value is the message that they both communicate. Remember to communicate excellence, legacy, and impact in all you do.

Summary

Giving back is a powerful way to contribute to the well-being of others and leave a lasting legacy that extends beyond your professional achievements. Individuals can make a meaningful difference in their communities and the world by identifying ways to contribute, mentoring, supporting others, creating sustainable change, leaving a lasting legacy, and celebrating the impact of giving back. Embrace the opportunity to give back and leave a positive legacy that inspires and empowers others to create a better future for all.

Career Mastery Exercise

Understanding the Power of Giving Back

- **Reflect:** What personal experiences have shaped your understanding of giving back and contributing to the community? How have these experiences influenced your values and actions?
- **Action:** Identify one cause or community initiative that resonates with you. Make a plan to volunteer your time or resources to this cause within the next month.
- **Action:** Write down three ways your current skills and expertise can benefit others. Consider how you can leverage these skills to make a positive impact.

Identifying Ways to Contribute

- **Reflect:** What are your passions and interests? How can they align with potential opportunities to give back to your community?
- **Action:** Create a list of local nonprofits, charities, or community organisations that align with your values. Reach out to at least one organisation to learn how you can get involved.
- **Action:** Set a goal to donate a specific amount of money, goods, or services to a meaningful cause this year. Track your contributions and the impact they have.

Mentoring and Supporting Others

- **Reflect:** Think about a mentor or supporter who has significantly impacted your life. What qualities made them effective, and how can you emulate these qualities in your mentoring?
- **Action:** Identify a mentee or someone you can support in your professional or personal network. Offer your guidance, share your experiences, and set regular check-ins to track their progress.
- **Action:** Develop a mentoring plan that outlines your goals, expectations, and the support you will provide. Share this plan with your mentee to ensure mutual understanding and commitment.

Creating Sustainable Change

- **Reflect:** Consider the long-term impact you want to have on your community or industry. What systemic issues do you feel passionate about addressing?

- **Action:** Conduct a PESTLE analysis to understand the broader factors influencing your community or industry. Use this analysis to identify opportunities for creating sustainable change.
- **Action:** Collaborate with others to develop a strategic plan for addressing a specific issue in your community. Outline actionable steps and measurable goals to track your progress.

Leaving a Lasting Legacy

- **Reflect:** What do you want to be remembered for? How do you want your contributions to impact future generations?
- **Action:** Create a vision statement for your legacy. This statement should reflect your values, goals, and the lasting impact you wish to leave.
- **Action:** Identify projects or initiatives that align with your vision statement. Develop a plan to start or support these initiatives, ensuring they contribute to your desired legacy.

Celebrating the Impact of Giving Back

- **Reflect:** Think about the impact you have already made in your community or industry. How can you celebrate and share these achievements to inspire others?
- **Action:** Document your journey of giving back, including the challenges, successes, and lessons learned. Share your story through blogs, social media, or community events to inspire others.
- **Action:** Recognise and celebrate the contributions of others in your community. Highlight their efforts and collaborate to amplify the impact of giving back.

Maintaining Balance and Well-being

- **Reflect:** How do you currently balance your professional, personal, and philanthropic commitments? Are there areas where you could improve?
- **Action:** Schedule regular self-care activities to ensure you maintain your physical, emotional, and mental health. Consider activities such as exercise, meditation, or spending time with loved ones.
- **Action:** Set boundaries to manage your time effectively and prevent burnout. Prioritise tasks and delegate responsibilities when necessary to maintain a healthy work-life balance.

CELEBRATING SUCCESS

*Reflecting on Your Achievements and
Finding Joy in Your Career Mastery*

Introduction

In pursuing career mastery, pausing and celebrating the milestones and successes along the way is essential. This section explores the significance of celebrating success, reflecting on achievements, and finding joy in your journey towards career mastery.

"Gratitude makes sense of our past, brings peace for today, and creates a vision for tomorrow."

- Melody Beattie

The Importance of Celebration

Celebrating success is not just about acknowledging achievements; it's about recognising the hard work, dedication, and perseverance that led to those accomplishments. Celebration boosts morale, fosters a sense of accomplishment, and reinforces positive behaviours and attitudes. It also provides an opportunity for reflection and gratitude, reminding us of how far we've come and motivating us to strive for excellence. I have earlier alluded to the importance of having a balanced mindset when you succeed and when you fail, referencing the popular quote from Anthony Joshua: "Do not let success get to your head, or failure get to your heart." That being said, an important component of attaining mastery is recognising feats and achievements in your life. Have you ever wondered why you need a graduation ceremony after obtaining a degree or an award of recognition after exceeding performance targets? The reason is not just to provide proof of achievement but to motivate you to remember those rewarding moments and to push harder for something bigger and better. I celebrate my successes in different ways, from a formal gathering of family and friends to taking myself out on a treat or buying something I have always wanted. Nonetheless, the bottom-line is that appreciation is the application to do more, so why not appreciate yourself to inspire yourself to do more for yourself?

Reflecting on Achievements

Take time to reflect on your achievements and milestones, both big and small. Celebrate not only major accomplishments but also progress, growth, and moments of triumph along the way. Reflect on the challenges you've overcome, the lessons you've learned, and the personal and professional growth you've experienced. Use reflection as an opportunity for self-awareness, appreciation, and learning, and let it fuel your motivation and drive for future success. Most academic courses in today's world incorporate reflections as part of their modules because that is one way of ensuring learning has taken place. As a lecturer, I ensure that the feedback I give my students borders around the areas of things they did well, things they could do better, and an action plan forward. Until you allow yourself to introspect and pick out these key areas after every milestone you achieve, you will most likely not make the best of every situation you find yourself in. Again, I cannot identify how well my clothes fit or notice any imperfections without looking into the mirror. Reflections are like a mirror that helps you step out of yourself for a moment and examine yourself through an unbiased lens, ultimately leading to growth and development.

Finding Joy in Your Journey

Amidst the pursuit of career mastery, it's essential to find joy and fulfilment in your journey. Identify aspects of your work that bring you joy, passion, and fulfilment, and prioritise those in your daily life. Whether solving complex problems, collaborating with others, or positively impacting others, find ways to cultivate joy and meaning in your work. Embrace the moments of flow, creativity, and inspiration that energise and uplift you, and let them fuel your passion and purpose. One thing that fulfils me at the end of every day is when I think back and realise that I have positively impacted someone or solved a complex problem. It fills me with some sense of joy, pride, and purpose, which gets me fired up for the next day. One of the ways you can kill your self-esteem is by not identifying what brings you the utmost joy and fulfilment in your life and striving to make that a daily occurrence. As I mentioned earlier, it does not have to be a massive feat all the time; just kind gestures to put a smile on someone's face can be the difference between feeling fulfilled and not. I remember when I was at the gym on a certain occasion, a young lady missed her steps while performing an exercise and banged her head on the floor. Some people at the gym had an awkward look on their faces, while some even laughed at her. She was having some sort of seizure afterwards, and as I was first aid trained, I stepped in to help her until the ambulance came around and thanked me for holding the fort, as she might have had some serious implications if I did not act on time. I went back home that day, saying to myself that if that were all I had achieved that day, I would be satisfied. Even better, I got to use a skill I acquired as part of my professional development to help someone in distress.

Expressing Gratitude and Appreciation

Express gratitude and appreciation for the support, guidance, and opportunities contributing to your success. Thank mentors, colleagues, friends, and family members who have played a role in your journey and acknowledge the contributions of others with sincerity and gratitude. Cultivate a culture of appreciation and recognition within your organisation, celebrating the achievements of individuals and teams and fostering a sense of camaraderie and collaboration. I will go back to an occasion when I was discussing with my wife just before we got married, and I told her that in our marriage, we should practise more appreciation than expectation. One reason is that expectation breeds a sense of entitlement for things to happen and disappointment when they don't. However, appreciation aims to celebrate every little positive and kind gesture that might naturally go unnoticed. What this does is that it motivates the person to do even more and fosters a healthier relationship between the parties involved. As a professional who has obviously received some guidance and assistance from people within your network, you must take the time to celebrate these people. It could be a random call to check in on them, buying them gifts on their birthdays, or even giving testimonials of them when recounting your achievements. According to Voltaire, "Appreciation is a wonderful thing. It makes what is excellent in others belong to us as well." Likewise, in the words of Melody Beattie, "Gratitude makes sense of our past, brings peace for today, and creates a vision for tomorrow."[44]

Sharing Successes and Inspiring Others

Share your successes and achievements with others to celebrate your accomplishments and inspire and motivate others on their own journeys. Be generous in sharing your knowledge, experiences, and insights with others, and serve as a role model and mentor for those who aspire to follow in your footsteps. By sharing your successes and celebrating the achievements of others, you contribute to a culture of positivity, growth, and excellence in your

---

[44] Parade, '50 Thankful Quotes for Practicing Gratitude All Year Long', Parade, 21 November 2023, https://parade.com/937289/parade/thankful-quotes/.

community and beyond. I must distinguish between rubbing your achievements in people's faces instead of sharing to inspire. If not done properly, you might more likely demotivate people you share your successes with. When you share your successes, be willing to follow up with steps you took to achieve them. Do not make it look like others are inferior to you, or no one can achieve what you have done. Instead, make it so that you aspire for what you have done to be replicated and even bettered. That does not in any way take away from what you have done, but instead lends credence to the effectiveness and efficiency of your mentorship and guidance. Also, ensure that sharing your stories with people who have similar beginnings to yourself offers them more belief and drive to see someone they can relate to. That could be in the form of students whose course you had studied, a professional level which you had been in the past, a project you had worked on, a challenge you had navigated, etc. When done properly, sharing your success could be one of the most effective ways of inspiring upcoming professionals or the next generation to strive for better.

Summary

Celebrating success is essential to finding joy and fulfilment in your journey towards career mastery. By reflecting on your achievements, finding joy in your work, expressing gratitude and appreciation, and sharing successes with others, you cultivate a sense of fulfilment, purpose, and meaning in your career. Embrace the opportunity to celebrate your successes and let them inspire and motivate you to continue striving for excellence and positively impacting your field and the world.

Career Mastery Exercise

The Importance of Celebration

- **Reflect:** Think about your recent accomplishments. What were the key factors that led to your success? How did you feel when you achieved these milestones?
- **Action:** Plan a celebration for a recent achievement. It could be a small gathering with friends, a personal treat, or simply taking time to acknowledge and appreciate your hard work.

Reflecting on Achievements

- **Reflect:** List the challenges you've overcome and the lessons you've learned from them. How have these experiences contributed to your personal and professional growth?
- **Action:** Set aside time each month to reflect on your progress. Write down your achievements, big and small, and consider how they align with your long-term goals.

Finding Joy in Your Journey

- **Reflect:** Identify the aspects of your work that bring you the most joy and fulfilment. What activities make you feel energised and motivated?
- **Action:** Incorporate more of these joyful activities into your daily routine. Prioritise tasks and projects that align with your passions and bring you satisfaction.

Expressing Gratitude and Appreciation

- **Reflect:** Think about the people who have supported and guided you in your journey. How have their contributions impacted your success?
- **Action:** Reach out to these individuals and express your gratitude. This could be through a heartfelt message, a thank-you note, or a small gift to show your appreciation.

Sharing Successes and Inspiring Others

- **Reflect:** Consider how sharing your successes can inspire others. What key insights and experiences can you share to help others on their journey?
- **Action:** Find a platform to share your story. This could be through writing a blog post, giving a talk, or mentoring someone who aspires to follow in your footsteps.

Maintaining Balance and Well-being

- **Reflect:** Assess your current work-life balance. Are there areas where you feel overwhelmed or neglected?
- **Action:** Create a self-care plan that includes activities to relax and recharge. Schedule regular breaks, exercise, and hobbies that bring you joy and relaxation.

CONCLUSION

YOUR JOURNEY, YOUR MASTERY

— · —

*Embracing the Path from Student
to Expert in Your Chosen Career*

Introduction

Embarking on the journey from student to expert in your chosen career is an exciting and fulfilling endeavour. This section examines the significance of embracing your unique journey towards mastery, navigating challenges, and seizing opportunities for growth and development along the way.

Embracing Your Unique Journey

Your journey towards mastery is uniquely yours, shaped by your experiences, passions, and aspirations. Embrace the uniqueness of your path and recognise that there is no one-size-fits-all approach to achieving mastery in your career. Embrace diversity, curiosity, and exploration as you navigate your journey, and trust in your ability to carve out a path that aligns with your values, interests, and goals.

Setting Intentions and Goals

Set clear intentions and goals for your career journey, outlining what you hope to achieve and the steps you will take to get there. Define your vision of success and identify milestones and objectives that will help you progress towards your goals. Break down your goals into manageable steps and prioritise actions that will move you closer to mastery in your chosen field.

Navigating Challenges and Setbacks

Challenges and setbacks are inevitable on the journey towards mastery but also present opportunities for growth and learning. Embrace challenges as opportunities to stretch and develop your skills, resilience, and perseverance. Approach setbacks with a growth mindset, viewing them as temporary obstacles that can be overcome with determination and resilience. Seek support from mentors, peers, and resources to help you navigate challenges and stay on course towards your goals.

Seizing Opportunities for Growth

Be proactive in seeking opportunities for growth and development in your career journey. Take on new challenges, projects, and responsibilities that allow you to stretch and expand your skills and knowledge. Seek mentorship, training, and learning opportunities that align with your interests and goals and be open to feedback and constructive criticism that helps you grow and evolve professionally.

Cultivating Resilience and Adaptability

Cultivate resilience and adaptability as you navigate the ups and downs of your career journey. Embrace change as a natural part of the learning process, and be willing to pivot and adapt your strategies in response to new opportunities and challenges. Cultivate a growth mindset, focusing on continuous learning and improvement, and trust your ability to overcome obstacles and thrive in adversity.

Celebrating Milestones and Achievements

Take time to celebrate milestones and achievements along the way, acknowledging your progress and the hard work and dedication it took to get there. Celebrate not only major accomplishments but also small victories and moments of growth and learning. Use celebration as an opportunity for reflection, gratitude, and renewed motivation to continue your journey towards mastery.

Summary

Your journey towards mastery is a unique and rewarding adventure filled with challenges, opportunities, and growth. Embrace the path that lies before you, setting clear intentions and goals, navigating challenges with resilience and adaptability, and seizing opportunities for growth and development along the way. Celebrate your achievements and milestones, and trust in your ability to continue progressing towards mastery in your chosen career. Embrace the journey, savour the experiences, and enjoy the fulfilment that comes from pursuing your passions and realizing your full potential.

REMEMBERING YOUR WHY

Staying True to Your Passion and Purpose Throughout Your Career

Introduction

In the hustle and bustle of a career, it's easy to lose sight of why you started in the first place. This section explains the importance of remembering your why—your passion and purpose—and staying true to it throughout your career journey.

Defining Your Why

Your why is the driving force behind your career choices, rooted in your passion, values, and sense of purpose. Take time to reflect on what motivates and inspires you and identify the deeper meaning and purpose behind your work. Your why serves as your guiding light, helping you stay focused, motivated, and fulfilled in your career.

Aligning Your Career with Your Values

Ensure that your career aligns with your values and beliefs and that you work towards meaningful and fulfilling goals. Consider how your work contributes to the greater good and aligns with your personal values and sense of purpose. When your career aligns with your values, you are more likely to feel fulfilled and satisfied in your work.

Finding Meaning in Your Work

Look for opportunities to find meaning and purpose in your everyday work, regardless of your role or position. Find ways to connect your work to a larger purpose or mission and focus on your impact on others and the world around you. Seek projects and initiatives that resonate with your values and passions and allow you to contribute your unique talents and strengths.

Navigating Career Transitions

During times of transition or uncertainty in your career, it's important to reconnect with your why and stay true to your passion and purpose. Use your why as a compass to guide your decisions and navigate challenges and obstacles. Trust your intuition and inner wisdom, and believe that staying true to your passion and purpose will lead you in the right direction.

Cultivating Resilience and Perseverance

Staying true to your passion and purpose requires resilience and perseverance in the face of adversity and setbacks. Cultivate resilience by embracing challenges as opportunities for growth and learning and maintaining a positive mindset and outlook. Draw strength from your why, and let it fuel your determination and perseverance during difficult times.

Reconnecting with Your Why

Regularly reconnect with your why to stay grounded and inspired in your career journey. Take self-reflection and introspection, and revisit your values, passions, and purpose. Surround yourself with people and environments that support and reinforce your why, and seek out experiences that ignite your passion and sense of purpose.

Summary

Remembering your why is essential for staying true to your passion and purpose throughout your career journey. By defining your why, aligning your career with your values, finding meaning in your work, navigating transitions with resilience, and regularly reconnecting with your why, you can stay focused, motivated, and fulfilled in your career. Embrace your why as your guiding light and let it lead you towards a meaningful, purposeful, and aligned career with who you are and what you value most.

THE WORLD AWAITS

— • —

Go Forth and Master Your Destiny!

Final Words

As you conclude this journey from student to master in your chosen career, the world stands before you, brimming with endless possibilities and opportunities. With knowledge, skills, and a passion for excellence, you are ready to embark on the next chapter of your life's journey with confidence, purpose, and determination.

Embracing Your Potential

You have honed your craft, overcome challenges, and celebrated successes along the way, but your journey towards mastery is far from over. Embrace your potential and believe in the limitless possibilities that lie ahead. Your expertise and unique talents can shape the future, inspire others, and impact your field and beyond.

Seizing Opportunities for Growth

As you step into the world as a master in your field, seize every opportunity for growth and learning that comes your way. Embrace challenges as opportunities to stretch and develop your skills and approach new experiences with curiosity, enthusiasm, and an open mind. Continuously seek opportunities to expand your knowledge, broaden your horizons, and push the boundaries of what you thought possible.

Making a Difference

Your journey towards mastery is not just about personal achievement; it's about making a difference in the world and leaving a lasting legacy. Use your expertise, influence, and passion to contribute to the greater good through innovation, mentorship, advocacy, or philanthropy. Leave a positive impact on the lives of others and inspire future generations to follow in your footsteps.

Embracing the Unknown

As you venture forth into the unknown, embrace the uncertainty and unpredictability of the journey ahead. Embrace change as an opportunity for growth and adaptation, and trust in your ability to navigate challenges and overcome obstacles along the way. Stay true to your values, passions, and purpose, and let them guide you towards fulfilment and success in your endeavours.

Fulfilling Your Destiny

The world awaits your unique talents, contributions, and insights. Go forth with courage, determination, and purpose, knowing you can shape your destiny and make a difference in the world. Embrace the journey of mastery with an open heart and a curious mind, and let it lead you towards a future filled with purpose, fulfilment, and endless possibilities.

I am Rooting for You!!!

As you close this chapter of your journey from student to master, remember that the world awaits your brilliance, passion, and potential. Go forth with confidence, courage, and conviction, and master your destiny with purpose and determination. Embrace the challenges, seize the opportunities, and leave a lasting legacy, inspiring and uplifting others for generations. The world is yours to conquer, so go forth and make your mark on the world. Your journey toward mastery has only just begun.

REFERENCES

Anthony Joshua [@anthonyjoshua]. '"One More Hour, One More Day, 25/8. Never Let Success Get to Your Head, or Failure to Your Heart." These Are Words I Live by and Inspiration for My New #BOSSxAJBXNG Collection. Take a Look at the New Pieces I Co-Created with the @HUGOBOSS Team #BOSSsports Https://On.Boss.Com/BOSSxAJBXNG_AJ_ Https://T.Co/BK0xtMC8MU'. Tweet. *Twitter*, 2 September 2020. https://x.com/anthonyjoshua/status/1301144318347014144.

Arsenal FC. 'Arteta on the Importance of Providing Energy'. Arteta on the importance of providing energy, 10 February 2023. https://www.arsenal.com/news/arteta-importance-providing-energy.

Beaty, Roger E. 'The Creative Brain'. *Cerebrum: The Dana Forum on Brain Science* 2020 (1 January 2020): cer-02-20.

Belbin, Meredith. 'The Nine Belbin Team Roles', 1981. https://www.belbin.com/about/belbin-team-roles.

Bible, Holy. 'New Living Translation'. *Gift and Award Edition*, 1996.

Bible, King James. *King James Bible*. Vol. 19. Proquest LLC, 1996.

Bloom, B. 'Bloom's Taxonomy of Learning', 1982.

Clausius, Rudolf. 'I. on the Moving Force of Heat, and the Laws Regarding the Nature of Heat Itself Which Are Deducible Therefrom'. *The London, Edinburgh, and Dublin Philosophical Magazine and Journal of Science* 2, no. 8 (1851): 1–21.

Collins. 'A Quote by Phil Collins', 2024. https://www.goodreads.com/quotes/32942-in-learning-you-will-teach-and-in-teaching-you-will.

Diamandis, Peter H, and Steven Kotler. *Bold: How to Go Big, Create Wealth and Impact the World*. Simon and Schuster, 2015.

Epic Gardening. 'Rose Growth Stages: How Fast Do Roses Grow?', 2023. https://www.epicgardening.com/rose-growth-stages/.

Future Learn. 'SMART Goals and Effectiveness'. *FutureLearn* (blog). Accessed 8 August 2024. https://www.futurelearn.com/info/blog.

Gale, Porter. *Your Network Is Your Net Worth: Unlock the Hidden Power of Connections for Wealth, Success, and Happiness in the Digital Age*. Simon and Schuster, 2013.

Gardening Express. 'Care Guide: Growing Palm Trees in British Gardens'. Gardening Express Knowledge Hub, 2023. https://help.gardeningexpress.co.uk/knowledge-base/how-to-grow-palm-trees/.

Garvey, Patrick. 'Making Sense of a Hero's Motivation'. Ancient Heroes, 2015. http://ancientheroes.net/blog/reconsidering-a-heros-motivation.

Grantham, Nick. 'Bloom's Taxonomy Verbs - Free Chart and Handout- Fractus Learning'. https://www.fractuslearning.com/, 25 January 2016. https://www.fractuslearning.com/blooms-taxonomy-verbs-free-chart/.

How To Get The Most Out Of 4 Levels Of Value, 2023. https://www.youtube.com/watch?v=_kdpDuoDjvA.

Lally, Phillippa, Cornelia H. M. van Jaarsveld, Henry W. W. Potts, and Jane Wardle. 'How Are Habits Formed: Modelling Habit Formation in the Real World'. *European Journal of Social Psychology* 40, no. 6 (1 October 2010): 998–1009. https://doi.org/10.1002/ejsp.674.

Landale, Anthony. 'Anyone Can Make a Bigger Difference'. *Manager*, 2010, 28.

Locke, Adriana. 'Adriana Locke Quotes (Author of Crank)', 2024. https://www.goodreads.com/author/quotes/8379774.Adriana_Locke.

Malik, Eddy. 'Amazon History Timeline', 2017. https://www.officetimeline.com/blog/amazon-history-timeline.

McCauley, CD, V Pollman, D Bracken, M Dalton, and R Jako. 'Should 360-Degree Feedback Be Used Only for Developmental Purposes'. *Ix-Xii*. *Greensboro, NC: Center for Creative Leadership*, 1997.

Microbe Safari. 'Cheese and Yoghurt'. *Microbe Safari* (blog). Accessed 12 August 2024. https://microbe-safari.org.uk/food-production/cheese-and-yoghurt-production/.

Munroe, Myles. *The Principle and Power of Kingdom Citizenship: Keys to Experiencing Heaven on Earth*. Destiny Image Publishers, 2016.

Murakami, Haruki. 'A Quote from Norwegian Wood', 2024. https://www.goodreads.com/quotes/621244-all-of-us-are-imperfect-human-beings-living-in-an.

Nathans-Kelly, Steve. 'Live Sports Streaming and the Edison Tone Test.' *Streaming Media* 21, no. 1 (2024): 3–4.

NIKE. 'NIKE, Inc.', 2024. https://about.nike.com/en.

Parade. '50 Thankful Quotes for Practicing Gratitude All Year Long'. Parade, 21 November 2023. https://parade.com/937289/parade/thankful-quotes/.

Radcliffe, Steve. *Leadership: Plain and Simple*. Pearson UK, 2012.

Sanders, M, and JMC Cormick. 'Human Factors in Engineering and Design. New York: McHill', 1993.

Sarfraz, Zouina, Azza Sarfraz, Hamza Iftikar, and Ramsha Akhund. 'Is COVID-19 Pushing Us to the Fifth Industrial Revolution (Society 5.0)?' *Pakistan Journal of Medical Sciences* 37 (4 January 2021). https://doi.org/10.12669/pjms.37.2.3387.

Singh, Avadhesh Kumar. 'Gandhian Values in the 21 St Century'. *Indian Literature* 63, no. 5 (313 (2019): 163–72.

Stumbles, Tim. 'History of Facebook Timeline', 2018. https://www.officetimeline.com/blog/facebook-history-timeline.

Sullivan, George H. *Not Built in a Day: Exploring the Architecture of Rome*. Da Capo Press, 2006.

Thembekwayo, Vusi. *Business & Life Lessons from a Black Dragon*. Tafelberg, 2018.

Umeokafor, Nnedinma, David Isaac, Keith Jones, and Boniface Umeadi. 'Enforcement of Occupational Safety and Health Regulations in Nigeria: An Exploration'. *European Scientific Journal* 3 (2014): 93–104.

Wise, Kim. '20 Inspiring Mentoring Quotes', 2020. https://www.mentorresources.com/mentoring-blog/20-inspiring-mentoring-quotes.

Yang, Yang. 'TikTok/Douyin Use and Its Influencer Video Use: A Cross-Cultural Comparison between Chinese and US Users'. *Online Media and Global Communication* 1, no. 2 (2022): 339–68.

ABOUT THE AUTHOR

Dr. Chizaram Nwankwo is the MD/CEO of Nancheez Ltd, a consultancy based in the UK which provides health and safety consultancy services to SMEs and multinational corporations.

A seasoned Health, Safety, Environmental and Human Factors expert based in the United Kingdom, Dr. Chizaram possesses a decade of diversified experience across industries such as oil and gas, healthcare, manufacturing, logistics, IT, and education. He is a Chartered/ Registered Member of the Chartered Institute of Ergonomics and Human Factors (CIEHF) also holding a PhD in Health and Safety & Human Factors. He is also an Associate Fellow of the Higher Education Academy in the United Kingdom. He has contributed significantly to the field, publishing numerous peer-reviewed journals, and working on complex industry projects on human factors, as well as health and safety across diverse industries, including Public Health England (PHE), the UK Health Security Agency (UKHSA) and the UK Defence Science and Technology Laboratory (DSTL).

He is a leader, visionary, mentor, public speaker, and nation builder who has impacted the lives of many professionals within and outside the shores of Africa and Europe.

Dr. Chizaram is happily married to Mrs. Chisomuaga Nwankwo and have a lovely daughter, Avielle together. They are a Christian family whose love for God transcends the shores of ministry, career, music, and business.

Engage further with Dr. Chizaram on the following platforms: -

 www.drchizaramnwankwo.com

 info@drchizaramnwankwo.com

 @dr_chizaram

 Dr. Chizaram Nwankwo

 Dr. Chizaram Nwankwo

JOURNAL PUBLICATIONS BY THIS AUTHOR

- Theophilus, S.C., Nwankwo, C.D., Acquah-Andoh, E., Bassey, E., Umoren, U., 2018. Integrating Human Factors (HF) into a Process Safety Management System (PSMS). Proc. Safety Prog. 37, 67–85. Available at: https://doi.org/10.1002/prs.11909

Human factors and process safety management (PSM) have become key factors in preventing exposure to both hazardous materials and major accidents. Therefore, comprehensive process safety management is required to address all aspects of human factors. Currently, there are several-process safety management models all of which have some weaknesses with respect to the control of human factors inherent in the process industry. Moreover, there is as yet no universally accepted process safety management model that treats process safety management as an integral part of the management system. Therefore, a need has arisen to integrate human factors and the existing frameworks and models into a single integrated management system to ensure a holistic approach of control and a continuous learning system. This article identifies the missing human factors in the current system and describes an integrated process safety management system (IPSMS) model drawn from screening all existing PSM frameworks, while integrating the Human Factors Analysis and Classification System (HFACS). The model, which adopts the PLAN, DO, CHECK, and ACT framework, also outlines an implementation strategy. We conclude that IPSMS provides both a theoretical and a practical framework with which to manage, measure and analyse process safety management systems. © 2017 American Institute of Chemical Engineers Process Process Saf Prog 37:67–85, 2018

- Nwankwo, C.D., Theophilus, S.C., Arewa, A.O., 2020. A comparative analysis of process safety management (PSM) systems in the process industry. Journal of Loss Prevention in the Process Industries 66, 104171. Available at: https://doi.org/10.1016/j.jlp.2020.104171

The root cause of most accidents in the process industry has been attributed to process safety issues ranging from poor safety culture, lack of communication, asset integrity issues, lack of management leadership and human factors. These accidents could have been prevented with adequate implementation of a robust process safety management (PSM) system. Therefore, the aim of this research is to develop a comparative framework which could aid in selecting an appropriate and suitable PSM system for specific industry sectors within the process industry. A total of 21 PSM systems are selected for this study and their theoretical frameworks, industry of application and deficiencies are explored. Next, a comparative framework is developed using eleven key factors that are applicable to the process industry such as framework and room for continuous improvement, design specification, industry adaptability and applicability, human factors, scope of application, usability in complex systems, safety culture, primary or secondary mode of application, regulatory enforcement, competency level, as well as inductive or deductive approach. After conducting the comparative analysis using these factors, the Integrated Process Safety Management System (IPSMS) model seems to be the most robust PSM system as it addressed almost every key area regarding process safety. However, inferences drawn from study findings suggest that there is still no one-size-fits-all PSM system for all sectors of the process industry.

- Nwankwo, C.D., Arewa, A.O., Theophilus, S.C., Esenowo, V.N., 2021. Analysis of accidents caused by human factors in the oil and gas industry using the HFACS-OGI framework. International journal of occupational safety and ergonomics 1–13. Available at: https://doi.org/10.1080/10803548.2021.1916238

Objectives. Human factors have been identified as the most common causes of catastrophic accidents in the oil and gas industry. Therefore, this study aims to analyse human causal factors of accidents in the oil and gas industry using the human factors analysis and classification system for the oil and gas industry (HFACS-OGI) framework. This study involved quantitative data collection for 184 accident cases in the oil and gas industry that occurred from 2013 to 2017 from the International Association of Oil and Gas Producers (IOGP) database. The causal factors of these accidents were coded using the HFACS-OGI framework. Accident data were analysed using descriptive statistics and the $\chi2$ test. Study findings reveal that 23% of all accidents were recorded in 2013. Thirty-two percent of accidents occurred in Asia, while 69% of accidents were recorded in onshore locations. Contractors were involved in 86% of accidents, while 28% of accidents occurred during drilling, workover and well services. The contractor's work environment was the main human factor in 90% of accident cases. The HFACS-OGI framework proves to be a vital tool for robust accident analysis of human factors in the oil and gas industry.

- Arewa, A.O., Ahmed, A., Edwards, D.J., Nwankwo, C., 2021. Fire Safety in High-Rise Buildings: Is the Stay-Put Tactic a Misjudgement or Magnificent Strategy? Buildings 11, 339. Available at:
https://doi.org/10.3390/buildings11080339

Historically, fire incidents in high-rise buildings reveal that Fire and Rescue Services frequently rely on the stay-put tactic (i.e., occupants of high-rise buildings should remain in their apartments) during an inferno. Recent fire occurrences in high-rise buildings reveal that there are two opposing viewpoints on the stay-put tactic. First, the understanding that the stay-put tactic is a beneficial practice used to protect, control, and facilitate smooth evacuation of occupants during fire incidents. Second, the argument that the stay-put tactic is a misjudgement and futile strategy that leads to fatalities, particularly in high-rise buildings. The aim of this study was to provide awareness and understanding of fire and rescue services use of the stay-put tactic in high-rise buildings. We attempted to answer the questions: is the stay-put tactic a misjudgement or magnificent strategy? The study adopted phenomenological research strategies with various focus groups consisting of seasoned firefighters and survivors with first-hand accounts of stay-put instructions in high-rise buildings. The study also scrutinised three case studies of fire incidents in high-rise buildings in two countries. The study revealed that the stay-put tactic is obsolete; with the potential to cause catastrophic misjudgement, mostly during conflagrations in high-rise buildings. There is a need to advance research on the use of artificial intelligence communication systems and infrared image detectors camera to enhance quick and smooth fire evacuation in high-rise buildings.

Keywords: fire and rescue services; high-rise buildings; stay-put tactic; fire safety

COMPARATIVE TITLES FOR THIS BOOK

If you loved reading Mastering your Career: A Guide from Student to Expert, the following books might also make amazing reads for you.

a. **"The Start-up of You: Adapt to the Future, Invest in Yourself, and Transform Your Career" by Reid Hoffman and Ben Casnocha**
   - This book focuses on managing and investing in one's career in a dynamic, ever-changing job market. It emphasises continuous learning, networking, and adaptability, which align closely with the themes of career development and mastery in Mastering your Career.

b. **"Lean In: Women, Work, and the Will to Lead" by Sheryl Sandberg**
   - While specifically addressing women, this book provides broader insights into leadership, career advancement, and overcoming professional challenges. The focus on building confidence and navigating a

career aligns well with the themes of personal and professional growth in Mastering your Career.

c. "So Good They Can't Ignore You: Why Skills Trump Passion in the Quest for Work You Love" by Cal Newport

- Newport's book emphasises the importance of skill development and deliberate practice over merely following one's passion. This aligns with the chapters in Mastering your Career that discuss building skills, developing expertise, and achieving mastery.

d. "Mindset: The New Psychology of Success" by Carol S. Dweck

- Dweck's exploration of the growth mindset and its impact on personal and professional success complements the themes in Mastering your Career about embracing continuous growth and learning. Her concepts about overcoming challenges and cultivating a resilient mindset are particularly relevant.

e. "Drive: The Surprising Truth About What Motivates Us" by Daniel H. Pink

- Pink's examination of what drives human motivation—autonomy, mastery, and purpose—parallels your book's focus on finding passion, setting goals, and pursuing career mastery. His insights into intrinsic motivation and career fulfilment provide a strong thematic match to Mastering your Career.